MW00984931

Deepening Your Effectiveness

"At a time when the church is struggling to understand what it means to make disciples for Jesus Christ, Dan Glover and Claudia Lavy have skillfully managed to put in our hands a road map that takes us to a place in the disciple-making process where we've never been before. *Deepening Your Effectiveness* is one of the most useful and dynamic resources in print today!"

Robert E. Hayes, Jr., Bishop Oklahoma Area
The United Methodist Church

"*Deepening Your Effectiveness* is a practical and down to earth description of how the church is able to impact the culture around it. The book offers practical, biblical insights into how to meet people where they are and invitationally encourage them to deepen their journey with Jesus."

George Howard, Director, Center for Congregational Vitality
West Ohio Conference

"Dan and Claudia bring creative, relevant, and life-changing ideas for making disciples. I highly recommend this book to all who want to lead others into a deeper commitment to the Lordship of Jesus."

John Perkins, Founder John M. Perkins Foundation for
Reconciliation and Development

Deepening Your Effectiveness

Restructuring the Local Church for Life Transformation

Dan Glover and Claudia Lavy

DISCIPLESHIP RESOURCES

P O BOX 340003 • NASHVILLE, TN 37203-0003
www.discipleshipresources.org

Cover design by Chris Gates and Shawn Lancaster.
Interior design by PerfecType, Nashville, TN.
Images by Chris Gates.

ISBN-13: 978-088177-475-7
ISBN-10: 0-88177-475-8

Library of Congress Control Number 2006929574

Contents

Introduction

Dan Glover

Growing up on the East Coast, the ocean played a significant role in my life. The long, hot summers of my childhood and adolescent years became the experiential filter through which my understanding of God and God's plan for turning ordinary men and women into life changers was processed. As I read stories in the Bible, real life experiences at the seashore would come to mind. For me, scripture makes sense in pictures, examples, and memories of where I've been and what I've done.

God, being the kind of guy he is, related to me personally as he revealed his discipleship plan in the form of ocean images. Each one called to mind an experience at the shore. The ocean diagram in this book collects these images and explains how people develop spiritually from unchurched to fully committed follower.

Once I understood how God does his transforming work, the challenge became how to apply that understanding in a tangible way in the local church. I'm a visionary, vision caster, and teacher. I can adequately get the job done, but implementation is not my strength. I needed someone to help turn the vision into a reality that carries with it a significant impact, so I prayed.

Claudia Lavy

As a teenager in my small Midwestern hometown, I watched the couple across the street, long time pillars of my church, gossip about everyone in town. I dreaded being near them for fear they would dredge up something hurtful to say about me. That's when I began to realize the church was not doing its job. There was a huge gap between what scripture said we were to be as followers of Christ and what those professing to be Christians actually were. It was obvious to me even then that lives were not being transformed and, in my experience, those living the abundant life that scripture promised were nowhere to be found. So, at age thirteen, I dropped out of church with no intention of going back to that house of hypocrites.

By twenty-eight, I realized we are all hypocrites to some degree, including me. With my personal life in chaos, I turned to the one whom, in my childhood, I had been told to trust in times of trouble. God saved me and set me on a journey that has taken me through extensive self-evaluation, as well as deep reflection on him. He revealed to me over many years that the church needed to restructure and be intentional about its mission. I'm a strong organizer and process thinker, so I understood how to develop a process that could move the church's product off the dock and to the consumer. Unfortunately, I wasn't quite sure what that product looked like, so I prayed. "Just tell me what you want me to do, Lord, and I'll do it," I said. Little did I know he would partner me in ministry with someone who had a product in need of a process.

CHAPTER ONE

The Ocean Diagram

In June of 1990, I had reached the end of eight and a half years that included a graduate seminary education, completion of the pastoral ministry process for my denomination and serving a second two-point charge. I was a fully ordained elder in the United Methodist Church, with all the rights and privileges that come with that position. However, in spite of all I had accomplished, something was not right and I couldn't quite put my finger on it. I was not in conflict with either of the local congregations I served. My relationship with the denomination was secure. I was not burnt out nor was I experiencing a crisis of belief. But I knew God was trying to show me something, and I finally came to realize it meant leaving the pulpit in order to discover the unknown.

During the weeks leading up to my last Sunday as a senior pastor, I felt like a hawk sitting atop a tree waiting to strike. The day had been closing in quickly and, now, it was just around the corner with one last sermon to preach. With a world of topics from which to choose, what does a preacher say when he's preparing his final message? I mentally sifted through the mound of personal encounters with men and women who had shared every facet of life with me until I landed on what I considered the most important topic facing the church: corporate worship. I didn't realize at the time that my passion for relevant, spirit-filled worship services as the doorway into the body of Christ for unchurched people would become the catalyst for a new understanding of discipleship and how people develop spiritually. I thought my life as a pastor was over but, with my love for God unshaken, surely God would use me elsewhere.

My family and I attended several different denominational churches, as well as a few independent ministries, as we shopped for a new church home. Fully immersed in secular work in order to pay the bills, I soon began to look at the church through the eyes of a visitor. I began to see with great clarity the plague of ineffective disciple making within the church. It became apparent that this ineffectiveness was not exclusive to the United Methodist denomination. It is rampant throughout the church and all have contributed to the demise of Christian influence on the cultural. God had put me in a position where I was able to see the church from a new perspective, ask deeper questions, and seek answers without the pressure of a senior pastor's weekly routine.

My first overarching question was and continues to be: "How did Jesus make disciples?" The second question is: "How do we duplicate what he did?" The pieces began to fall into place after a year and a half of asking and seeking. Scripture slowly exposed six identifiable stages of spiritual development in the midst of the very human story lived out by Jesus and those he encountered.

This picture of the ocean is the image through which I began to discover the progressive stages of spiritual development, and how the overall journey from seeking to becoming a fully committed follower fits into the life of the church. The six figures depict six distinct stages through which people develop a deeper and deeper trusting relationship with God. The ocean represents the body of Christ. The church, more than anything else, plays the most crucial role in their development. Ephesians 3:10 says, *"His intent was that now, through the church, the manifold wisdom of God should be made known to the rulers and authorities in the heavenly realms."* It is both our privilege and our responsibility as clergy and lay leaders in the church to make every effort to intentionally development people spiritually; in other words, to make disciples.

The Primary Elements of Each Stage

There are some "primaries" as people make their journey toward becoming a fully committed follower of Christ. At each stage there is a:

Primary person: The person on the spiritual journey, the traveler who is moving toward deeper water.

Primary question: The conscious or subconscious question that resonates in the heart and mind of the traveler, however, the question changes from stage to stage. These are the questions the ministries of the church must recognize and seek to answer, if we are to become effective disciple makers.

Primary relationship: The person who has the most influence when it comes to helping the traveler move forward into the next stage. It is the responsibility of the church to identify and capitalize on these relationships by intentionally providing opportunities for them to develop.

Primary barrier: Woven into the fabric of human nature are natural tendencies that guard us from the unknown. These tendencies, which can keep us from harm's way, can also act as barriers to our forward movement into God's unknown future for us. The purpose of the ministries of the church is to help the traveler overcome and move through these barriers.

Primary ministry: There is a primary ministry that can have a significant, positive impact on the traveler at each stage of development. The job of the church is to place emphasis on the creation and ongoing maintenance of these ministries in order to have maximum impact.

The first half of this book will be devoted to an explanation of each of the six stages. We will offer biblical examples of how each is revealed through the lives of New Testament characters, how Jesus addressed his disciples at each stage, and how they reproduced this disciple making in their relationships with others after Jesus' ascension.

For me, the ocean is a perfect analogy of the ebb and flow of everyday life and the deepening faith of a growing Christian. It not only reflects our movement from the shoreline into deeper water, but also our movement back and forth between stages as we encounter various victories, defeats, obstacles and challenges. In some cases, travelers venture into the deep water of the church too quickly, fall prey to the invisible but very real dangers inherent to the deep, and are damaged spiritually, only to have their dead bodies wash back on shore. Ultimately, the blame for that damage lies with the church that has not done the hard, unseen spiritual work of becoming a safe, intentional, disciple making place.

Jesus said in John 14:6, *"I am the way, the truth and the life. No one comes to the Father except through me."* If it is true that Jesus is the truth, then the church must be the keeper of the truth and must be led by women and men who are keepers of the truth, not merely doers of good things in the name of Jesus. While God has placed in each of us a natural desire to seek after truth, the church and its leaders must recognize and acknowledge that the journey toward truth is littered with obstacles and barriers. To the unsuspecting traveler who rushes deep into the journey without first being properly equipped by the church, the results can be disastrous. It is the responsibility of the church to mark, maintain, and point the way.

Jesus went on to say in John 14:7, *"If you really knew me, you would know my Father as well."* As people of the Great Commission, we have only one job: to fill our churches with people who, at the end of their lives, can say without a shadow of a doubt, "I really knew Jesus." When that happens, the world will not be able to contain the church. We will be everywhere, serving everyone and lifting up the name of Jesus as our motivation. It's possible. It's achievable. Jesus, who is Truth, would not have sent us to go and make disciples of all nations if we were not actually able to accomplish the mission. Let's look at how we can get the job done.

CHAPTER TWO

Stage One: Life on the Beach

My oldest daughter is now grown and married, but when she was in elementary school, I met one of her teachers at an open house. Hearing I was the pastor of a Christian church, she made a point to state up front that she was an atheist and, from my subsequent observations, seemed quite comfortable with that theological position. Our paths crossed several times throughout the year at various school related events. Each time we talked, our conversation invariably moved to spiritual matters. After months of exchange, she inquired about the church where I served on staff and asked what went on there. I explained there was music similar to what she probably listened to on the radio, a great preacher who talked like a regular guy and spoke of things that made sense to most people, familiar video clips, and lots of multi-media. I asked if she would like to come and see for herself. Because we had developed a trusting relationship, she accepted my invitation and scheduled a time to meet me at the church the following Sunday.

On Friday, she called. As soon as I heard her voice I thought, "Here we go. She's going to back out." Much to my surprise, she reiterated her interest and commitment to join my family at church and asked, "What exactly should I wear? Something formal, informal, casual, or what?" As it turned out, she was actually looking forward to seeing what church was all about and didn't want to feel out of place by wearing the wrong thing. My daughter's teacher decided I was trustworthy enough to accept my invitation to come and see what church might have to offer. As a result, she continued to attend that church for many years.

We established in chapter one that the illustration of the ocean represents the body of Christ, the church. The beach, then, represents the world. Those who dwell on it are disconnected from the church. Many are unchurched or unbelievers while others are previously churched or believers but, for various reasons, find themselves unable to relate to what the church offers them today. As a result, they are resistant to any spiritual development that holds potential value for them. Nevertheless, life on the beach is clearly the first stage of spiritual development to which scripture attests.

In Jesus' ministry there was an obvious emphasis placed on the men and women at this first stage. When asked why he associated with tax collectors and sinners, Jesus emphatically states in the book of Mark and again in Luke, *"It is not the healthy who need a doctor, but the sick. I have not come to call the righteous, but sinners, to repentance."* This response to the questioning of the Pharisees gives credible identity to those who are irreligious. Matthew 9:13a adds further dimension to his statement when Jesus said, *"But go and learn what this means: 'I desire mercy, not sacrifice.'"* This statement is a reference to Hosea 6, where the prophet informs Judah that God desires relationship, not religious ceremony or offerings. Jesus' reply to the Pharisees is an arrow pointing the way to the hearts and minds of those who are separated and disconnected from the church. We can reach them through mercy and grace demonstrated in relationships, not by persuading them to follow religious rules or buy into forms of outdated religious ceremony that are irrelevant to them. Too often, those who are disconnected from Christ come into our churches and are met by inappropriate actions and unrealistic expectations. An example is the visiting preacher who sat with the senior pastor near the lectern one Sunday morning. As the service moved through the order of worship, a liturgist stepped to the microphone and said, "Let's stand for the Lord's Prayer". The entire congregation stood up, turned around, faced the back of the church and recited the Lord's Prayer in unison. When they finished, they turned back around and took their seats. Curious about this unique practice, the visiting preacher assumed it must be a corporate act of humility. After the service, he asked the senior pastor, "Why did everyone turn around for the Lord's Prayer?" The senior pastor replied without hesitation, "Oh, for many years the Lord's Prayer was written on the back wall for those who could not remember it. Fifteen years ago we remodeled the sanctuary and painted over it, but the congregation never got out of the habit of turning around."

The disconnected were clearly the ones to whom Jesus continually exhorted his followers to preach, reach out, and minister. He talked of leaving the ninety-nine in search of one in the parable of the lost sheep. He illustrated his love for the disenfranchised by describing a woman with ten silver coins who lost one and swept the entire house until she found it. He described the joy of a father at the return of his wayward son. He spoke of serving, visiting, and feeding the least of these in Matthew 25. Jesus obviously had a passionate heart for the disconnected and disenfranchised. His words to his first followers, and to us as well, make room for them because they are close to his heart, just as those who already follow him are close to his heart. Jesus identified life outside the church—life on the beach—as the first stage of spiritual development.

The Unchurched Person

The primary person at stage one is the unchurched person. In workshops throughout the United States, we ask people, "If they think about the church at all, what question do you suppose runs through the mind of an unchurched person as he or she drives past a house of worship on Sunday morning?" The responses sound like this: "What goes on in there?" "Why would I go there? It's full of hypocrites." "What's in there for me?" "What interest would I possibly have in church?" "Would anyone there accept me?" These are credible responses, because they come from many who themselves were previously disconnected from the church. Summed up, the primary question on the heart and mind of the unchurched person is one of relevance, "Is this for real?"

Many unchurched people are on an honest search for the truth. They may look in all the wrong places, but their quest is sincere. Sadly, they have good reason to hesitate when it comes to seeking truth through the church. All too often the media, as well as our own personal experiences, remind us that the church does not live out the very truth it proclaims. Whether a particular account is accurate or not is inconsequential to a person in stage one. The message that is conveyed to the unchurched mind is that the church, in general, is not relevant to people living in today's culture. It has no real value and it makes no identifiable difference in your life or mine, so why bother? It's simply a waste of their time.

An Old Trusted Friend

However, there is a primary relationship in the life of that unchurched person that can cut to the heart of the question "Is this for real?" and help facilitate movement from stage one to the second stage of spiritual development. That primary relationship is an old trusted friend. You know who they are. They are the people we've known for years. We've grown up with them; they have come to our birthday parties, lived next door and watched us raise our children and mow our grass. They have observed our actions and reactions in the marketplace and when things don't go our way. We have had lunch and gone to the movies with them. Some have even shared their dreams with us. They are coworkers, relatives and neighbors, women and men who are part of our bowling league, PTA, and civic organization. They weave in and out of our personal lives in one way or another at various levels of involvement. They are the people with whom we have built trust.

This trust relationship is recorded in a conversation between Philip and Nathaniel in John 1:45. *"Philip found Nathaniel and told him, 'We have found the one Moses wrote about in the Law, and about whom the prophets also wrote, Jesus of Nazareth.'"* Here we have two long time friends engaged in a conversation about Jesus. Just prior to verse 45 we find that Philip was from the town of Bethsaida, a town north of Nazareth. Nathaniel was from the town of Cana, located between

Bethsaida and Nazareth. Later in the book of John, these same two men are fishing together along with Peter. We can surmise from these passages that Philip and Nathaniel probably grew up together in this cluster of tight knit fishing communities and were most likely fellow fishermen. Based on the account in John, they qualify as old trusted friends. They knew each other apart from any spiritual connection, and God used this relationship as the foundation on which enter Nathaniel's life.

Is This for Real?

Statistics say that most people don't attend church because they have never been invited. Again, this is a matter of relevance for them. They think, "If my old trusted friend doesn't invite me to church, it must not mean much to him. So what could it possibly mean to me?" Nathaniel's response to Philip's exclamation that he had found the messiah is recorded in John 1:46a. *"Nazareth? Can anything good come from there?"* It reflects Nathaniel's version of an unchurched person's primary question (Is this for real?) and questions the relevance of anything that might emerge from Nazareth.

Cynicism

When someone extends an invitation to an unchurched friend or relative to give church a try, there is an internal barrier that pops up. This barrier can keep him or her from moving toward God through the church. That barrier is cynicism. Left unaddressed, it will stop the person dead in his or her tracks. Those of us who have attempted to speak with our unchurched friends and family about the value of biblical community in the local church have more than likely run into the same cynicism that drips from Nathaniel's lips. "The church? Can anything good come from there?" Nazareth had no credibility with Nathaniel, and the church has no credibility with an unchurched person. What *does* have credibility with Nathaniel, however, is Philip, his old trusted friend, just as you and I have credibility with those who consider us their old trusted friend.

Come and See

When we look at John 1:46b, we see the sum total of Philip's evangelistic effort and outreach to Nathaniel. Faced with Nathaniel's raw cynicism, Philip simply says, "Come and see". That's all. He didn't whip out a tract and explain a set of spiritual laws. He didn't ask him if he was going to heaven or hell, or if he knew what the Torah said about life after death. All he said was, "Come and see." And in these words we have the foundation for the primary ministry to an unchurched person. It is a "come and see" ministry.

A come and see ministry is relevant enough to an unchurched person to make it worth his or her time and effort to come and see what it has to offer. There are numerous entry points into the church—youth ministry, singles ministry, children's ministry, small groups—and each one has the potential for becoming a "come and see" ministry. But the one ministry that traditionally serves as the main entry point into the life of a local congregation is worship, and it must be considered the come and see ministry with the highest priority. You may be thinking, "We have a worship service worth coming and seeing. Why, we have 225 people who come and see it every week!" But that 225 are probably *churched* people. You cannot measure the effectiveness of your worship experience by counting those who are already committed to the church. Churched people, who have made an emotional investment in your congregation, will come to virtually anything the church offers! The acid test of an effective come and see worship ministry is whether or not your average attendee will stake his or her personal reputation among his unchurched friends and family on the quality of your worship experience and actually invite them.

Let's play out that scenario. Roger and Bill have been coworkers for five years. Roger has been attending your worship service for the past eighteen months. Bill has no prior church experience. He is somewhat cynical about Christians in general and the church in particular. One Monday over hamburgers at the local diner, Roger tells Bill about the great time he had the previous weekend at a retreat hosted by the men's ministry. Roger's excitement about his experience spills over, and Bill is intrigued and asks more questions. Recognizing Bill's piqued interest, Roger invites Bill to come with him to worship the following Sunday and see for himself. The week passes, and as they each head for home on Friday afternoon, Bill waves from his open car window and shouts, "See you Sunday!" And then Sunday morning arrives. Roger stands at the door of the church with butterflies in his stomach. His palms are sweaty. Second thoughts are running through his mind. "O God, I hope the pastor didn't throw his sermon together Saturday night! I hope the choir doesn't sing off key this week!" Why is Roger agonizing over his earlier decision to invite Bill to worship? Because Monday's coming! He knows he will have to face his buddy Monday morning, and hopefully his credibility will remain intact. Roger knows if the worship service was not something unchurched Bill finds worth the time and energy he expended to come and check it out, then Roger will be confronted with "the look." You know "the look." It's the one that says, "That was the biggest waste of time I've ever seen. Don't *ever* ask me to do that again!" Believe me! Roger not only will never ask Bill again, he also will never, ever ask anyone else! Why would he possibly run the risk of another blow to his credibility?

If the key to cynical unchurched people coming to Christ through your church is an old trusted friend like Roger or Philip, then this is a point you cannot afford to take lightly. Philip did not hesitate to invite Nathaniel because he was confident he had something to come and see that Nathaniel would consider relevant and meaningful. Roger, on the other hand, had reason for concern and began questioning his decision to invite Bill before the choir ever sang a note.

In chapter four of the book of John, Jesus is found traveling through Samaria on the west side of the Jordan River. There was great hostility between the Israelites and the Samaritans. Jews were regularly refused overnight lodging when traveling through Samaria on the three day journey between Galilee and Jerusalem, so they would typically cross to the east side of the Jordan to avoid conflict. But Jesus did not cross the river. Instead, he traveled undaunted through this extremely unfriendly environment. Opportunities for kingdom advancement in this place were slim. Jesus is tired and rests at Jacob's well. In verse 7, a Samaritan woman approaches the well to draw water and Jesus strikes up a conversation. "*Will you give me a drink?*" he asks. The conversation is awkward at first and focuses on simple things like water and thirst. But soon it begins to flow into deeper, more spiritual topics, until they finally engage in a conversation about the woman's lifestyle. The woman finds Jesus' message relevant and meaningful to her current reality. They connect through her cynicism about Jews and the barriers between Jew and Samaritan suddenly dissolve. She realizes she has encountered truth embodied in the person of Jesus. The disciples soon arrive at the well and are unaware, as they often were, of the invisible power of the moment. The scripture goes on to say, " . . . *leaving her water jar, (the woman) went back to town and said to the people, 'Come, see a man who told me everything I ever did.'*" What transpires in the next few verses is nothing short of a cross-cultural miracle that stems from the power of the "come and see" dynamic. The woman, after experiencing the relevant truth of Jesus, now becomes the old trusted friend who does not hesitate to invite her "unchurched" friends to meet him. They come to meet Jesus based on their trust in this woman because they have no trust in a traveling Jew. The come and see dynamic, when fully in motion, convicts the heart of the receiver that what he or she has witnessed is worth inviting others to experience. The receivers, in turn, go out and spread the word, convincing others to come and see as well. In this story, the "come and see" dynamic played out to its logical conclusion for the Samaritan townspeople. John 4:39 says, *"Many of the Samaritans from that town believed in him because of the woman's testimony . . ."* Just as Philip, the old trusted friend, had credibility with Nathaniel, the townspeople's trust in the Samaritan woman propelled them to come and see that Jesus was worth their time and energy. They were not disappointed and the door to faith was opened.

But it didn't stop there. Scripture shows us the entire picture of this incredible relational interplay. John 4:40-42 says, *"So when the Samaritans came to him, they urged him to stay with them, and he stayed two days. And because of his words, many more became believers. They said to the woman, 'We no longer believe just because of what you said: now we have heard for ourselves, and we know that this man really is the Savior of the world.'"* When the come and see dynamic is functioning in a healthy and effective way, there comes a moment when a relational transfer is made. The Samaritans came to see Jesus on the credibility of the woman, but his relevance to their individual lives caused a transfer of credibility from the woman at the well to this new person they encountered. Whether the townspeople realized it or not, they were moving from the cynicism of stage one to the curiosity that so aptly characterizes a person at stage two.

The primary components of stage one of the journey toward becoming a fully committed follower of Christ:

The primary person: Unchurched

The primary question: Is this for real?

The primary relationship: An old, trusted friend

The primary barrier: Cynicism

The primary ministry: Come and see

CHAPTER THREE

Stage Two: Life on the Shoreline

When I was a child, my family spent summer vacations in Nags Head, North Carolina. Images of surf and sand still blow across my mind and fond memories of the Outer Banks are securely embedded there.

From the first time I saw it, there was something about the ocean that drew me in. Even now, when I travel to the coast, I can be miles away and still find myself thinking, "Those clouds ahead are not over land. They are over the ocean." I watch the trees begin to thin out and feel the change in the roll of the land as the continent gives way to the sea. When the smell of salt fills the air, I know that just beyond the limits of my vision is the sight that will once again take my breath away. Gradually, the sounds of the ocean overtake the clamor of daily life. The cry of sea gulls replaces voices, and the pounding surf drowns traffic noise. Eventually, the only thing that separates me from that vast expanse of water is sand dunes. The anticipation I feel as I ascend the sandy slope reminds me of the excitement of Christmas morning. Finally, I reach the crest . . . and there it is! The ocean! I realize it's only water, but the grandeur and power of the sea never ceases to amaze me and I'm overwhelmed by a sense of awe.

I learned early on that there are two types of people who travel to the shoreline: those who vacation at the ocean and those who vacation at the beach. While my sister, Kathy, was a beach-dweller, I was definitely among those who vacation at the ocean.

I would race up the dunes, and just as I would reach the top, my clothes would begin flying in every direction. I'd strip down to my swim trunks and race straight across the beach toward the water. I would take increasingly larger steps as I approached the surf, hit the water and dive as high as I could over the next incoming wave. Once fully immersed, I had finally reached the invisible destination we call "vacation"!

Kathy had an entirely different approach. After tossing and tumbling my way through the waves for half an hour or more, I would see her casually strolling over the dunes. She would identify a spot on the beach where she would neatly place her towel on the sand, then stretch out to sunbathe for what seemed to me to be an eternity. Occasionally, I would call to her from the water, urging her to come in and have fun. Finally, she would rise up from her towel, survey the area around her, and begin to make her way toward the water. Kathy's idea of swimming was to walk up to the water's edge and let the surf wash across her feet and ankles. She would reach down and wiggle her fingertips in the water to test the temperature. And then the moment I had waited for arrived. It was the moment of crucial decision. I could hear the question running through her mind. "Do I go in the water with Dan and play, or go back to the beach and lay in the sun?" Of course, I wanted her to dive in. I had plans to swim under water and grab her ankle and splash water in her face, because this is the stuff of which dream vacations are made if you are a nine-year-old boy! After all, I could only entertain myself for so long before I needed my sister to pester.

Over time, I learned some important lessons from Kathy's moment of decision. If I yelled and insisted she come out and play, if I repeatedly tried to convince her that the water was fine, she would invariably head back to her beach towel. I learned that my exuberance actually had the opposite effect from what I desired. But, if I simply kept swimming and playing and demonstrated what a great time I was having out in the waves, the chance of her joining me dramatically increased. Of course, when she did decide to join me, I would quickly run her off because older sisters really don't like to be pestered by their little brothers.

Let's freeze frame the mental picture I just painted of my childhood trip to the shore. Notice the small and critical window of time I had to demonstrate that the best decision my sister could possibly make was to come into the water. The church has an equally small and critical window of time in which to demonstrate to spiritual "water testers" that it offers answers to their questions, direction for their lives, and healing for their hearts in Christ. I could tell my sister until I was blue in the face that this was the best body surfing I had ever seen, and it would mean nothing to her if she reached down to test the water and found it cold. Her assessment would tell her, "This doesn't feel good. I'm going back to the beach." Likewise, it doesn't matter to visitors whether the church has an acclaimed preacher, an amazing music ministry, state of the art multi-media or the greatest Sunday school offerings ever developed. At stage two of spiritual development, there is only one thing a person wants to know: Is the water of the church cold or warm? If it's warm, she will venture into deeper water. If it's cold, she's going to head back to the beach. The principles of stage two are all wrapped up in the shoreline interchange between my sister and me.

The Curious Person

The primary person at stage two is a curious person. He isn't swimming in the water of the church yet. He is simply approaching the shoreline to test water temperature. After responding to the invitation of old trusted friends, the biblical accounts of both Nathaniel and the Samaritans show that they became curious enough to get up off their proverbial towels and move to the water's edge where they could test the water. No commitment to swim, no life long profession of faith, just a visit to check it out for themselves.

A New Acquaintance

Let's look again at the story of Philip and Nathaniel. Philip had invited his cynical friend to come and see Jesus for himself. John 1:47 says, *"When Jesus saw Nathaniel approaching . . . "* Jesus was stationed at a place where he could see people arriving and was prepared to receive them. When he saw Philip and Nathaniel making their way through the parking lot toward the church lobby, he was ready to greet Nathaniel and become the primary relationship every curious person needs in order to move toward the next stage of spiritual development: a new acquaintance. Verse 47 goes on to say, *" . . . he (Jesus) said of him (Nathaniel), 'Here is a true Israelite, in whom there is nothing false.'"*

Heightened Sensitivity

There are three lessons to be learned from this passage. First, notice that Jesus doesn't talk to Philip. Instead, he talks to Nathaniel. Remember that Nathaniel is coming not because this man from Nazareth has credibility, but because Philip has credibility. At the moment Philip walks through the door with Nathaniel, he can't hold up a sign that says, "Will someone please talk to my friend so he knows that what I said about this place is true?" Jesus was ready and waiting to receive the handoff from Philip and help move Nathaniel into the presence of God in a way that is relevant to the curious person at stage two. Was Philip offended that Jesus didn't speak to him? Absolutely not! Philip had already made a commitment to Jesus, and together their goal was to spread the good news to others.

Second, Jesus had anticipated and was prepared for interaction with Nathaniel. Waiting at the front door for this first time visitor, Jesus was alert to the fact that he was about to become the new acquaintance that begins to give credibility to the church. He knew that this curious person was facing the primary barrier to further spiritual development: heightened sensitivity. Listen to Nathaniel's response to Jesus in verse 48. *"'How do you know me?' Nathaniel asked. Jesus answered, 'I saw you while you were still under the fig tree before Philip called you.'"* Can you hear his heightened sensitivity? "How could you possibly know me and why are you being so nice?" he asked. Jesus responded, "I've seen you before. Haven't I seen you mowing a lawn over on Walnut Street? Is that your house? I think our kids go to the same school." What Jesus did was build a bridge to Nathaniel by letting him know that they really were not as disconnected from each other as it seemed. Suddenly, disarmament began to take place and sensitivities were soothed.

Third, Jesus was authentic in his desire to convey Nathaniel's importance and value as a person. Jesus wasn't trying to be his buddy, he wasn't trying to work the crowd and greet everyone. Jesus practiced being fully present with the people who crossed his path. Authentic means original, the real deal, not counterfeit or copied. Jesus was all of that, and he calls his followers to be the same. We can train our front-line ministry servants in the how-to of completing their task, but authenticity comes from a commitment to be fully present with every person God brings across their path. They become life-changers when they commit to authenticity in their ministry. While a handshake might be enough to convince some that the water is warm, it may not be enough for others like Nathaniel who quickly asked, "How do you know me?" It's easy to smile and chirp, "Good morning!" to a visitor walking into the church for the first time, then quickly turn back to a friend and continue a conversation about last night's football game. This type of cold-water experience in the place that professes to offer real love and acceptance to everyone sends curious people scurrying back to the beach, never to be heard from again.

So important was Nathaniel's encounter with Jesus that he went on to become devoted to the Master and his teachings for the rest of his natural life. This pivotal moment in the process of making disciples cannot be over emphasized. The church must take advantage of the small and critical window of time to overcome and not ignore the heightened sensitivity of curious visitors. If we miss it, these spiritual "water testers" can be stopped dead in their tracks and discipleship, for them, grinds to a screeching halt. You know what happens next: They head back to the beach!

As embarrassing as it is, I'd like to tell a story on myself that shows how easy it is to lose focus and slip into behavior that destroys the church's credibility. Several years ago, I was teaching this very lesson on stage two to a group of men on Sunday morning. I broke the class into table groups to discuss the significance of authentic, high-impact hospitality and new acquaintance encounters and had a few minutes to slip into the hall for a drink of water. As I moved toward the water fountain, I spotted my friend, Bill, and his family filing through the crowded hallway toward the worship area for the service that was about to start. He waved to me and I noticed he had with him two people I didn't recognize. Bill and I exchanged greetings and he introduced me to his neighbors who were visiting our church for the first time. I politely shook their hands, told them how glad I was to meet them, then immediately turned back to Bill and picked up on a prior conversation we started earlier in the week. After a few minutes of conversation with Bill and Bill alone, I remembered that my table groups would be wrapping up their discussions. I needed to hurry back to the classroom so I said my goodbyes to Bill, his family and the neighbors whose names I had already forgotten and hustled down the hall toward my class. Oblivious to what I had just done, I returned to the men's group and continued discussing the importance of new acquaintance encounters with first time visitors. As the day wore on, the dawning realization that I had politely but completely ignored Bill's neighbors made me heartsick. I had been responsible for giving them a sample of what life in this church was going to be like. They were testing the water, and I helped them discover that it was cold as ice. I never got a second chance with Bill's neighbors, but to this day, I walk the lobby and halls of the church each Sunday morning making sure I'm available and present to the people God sends my way. I won't make that mistake again.

Authentic High Impact Hospitality

That being said, let's look at the primary ministry that will overcome the heightened sensitivity of people at stage two—authentic, high-impact hospitality. It exceeds the expectations of curious visitors, provides a "WOW" experience, and conveys the message, "We have been expecting you!" For hospitality to have a high impact, it has to be excellent hospitality, not just same old, same old. To exceed expectations, it has to offer something unexpected, something different than the rest, something that makes you say, "Wow!" To convey the message, "We've been expecting you!" it has to be designed with the visitor's needs in mind, not the convenience of the ministry servants who are charged with being hospitable. I'm sure you are mentally assessing the greeters who currently man the doors of your church in comparison to this criteria and you should. But hospitality extends far beyond greeters to include parking lot attendants, ushers, information desk servants, food service personnel, housekeeping, facilities and grounds maintenance, and signage. It includes every ministry that is responsible for creating a first impression. When a church strives to develop a culture of authentic, high-impact hospitality that permeates every frontline ministry, curious stage two people will find new acquaintances at every turn.

Excellence and Authenticity

Excellence and authenticity have been waging a silent war in the church for decades. There is an invisible line drawn between those who believe the church should look, act, and feel more modern and progressive, and those who believe progressing will turn worship into an irreverent performance and the leadership structure into an uncaring corporate beast. However, the battle exists in the hearts and minds of churched people only. Unchurched people aren't at war. For them, it's simple. If the church presents itself in a way that is less than excellent, unchurched people simply don't come. That presentation extends from the appearance of exterior signs and office hours that are convenient to them through frontline ministries to worship and children's ministry. We are competing for the discretionary time of people who do not attend church, and they will give it to the activities that best live up to their expectations.

Once they come and see, however, excellence alone will not keep them. They need authentic relationships in order to move to the next stage of development. We churched people can dispute this need for both excellence and authenticity as long as we want, but the men and women we are trying to reach have already spoken by their lack of desire to make church a part of their lives. We can be the most authentic church family in the world, but the unchurched will not come if we don't devote significant time and energy to excellence in all we do. By the same token, we can offer the most excellent worship service imaginable in a beautiful building that operates flawlessly, but the curious will not stay without connection to relationships with those who are living demonstrations of the authenticity of Christ. Therefore, the line in the sand that this ongoing argument has drawn is pointless. It's not either/or; it's both/and.

Somewhere in the numerous conferences and seminars I've attended over the past five years, I learned that people over the age of fifty (born before 1950) grew up in a culture that expected authenticity and was surprised by excellence, and people under the age of fifty (born after 1950) have grown up in a culture that expects excellence and is surprised by authenticity. When I heard this, my brain exploded with the implications of this statement in relation to stage two people who have come to see if the church has anything relevant to offer them. Churches that are not growing or affecting the community around them in any significant way typically have reached a plateau in attendance. Their membership usually consists of long time members, most over the age of fifty. They would like to have more young families join them, but the fact that no young families bother to visit confuses them. However, let's consider the statement I just made about expectations of authenticity (over age fifty), versus expectations of excellence (under age fifty). If this statement is true, then the view of the church by the over age fifty congregation is vastly different from the view of the church by the young, under age fifty families they hope to attract. It means much of what the existing church family considers attractive, inviting, and comfortable may actually be keeping visitors at arm's length.

Most stage two people who walk into the church are coming from a culture that has saturated them with expectations of excellence and perfection. Think about it: Disneyland opened fifty years ago this year and raised the bar for excellence in customer service and "wow" experiences. Most stage two people have grown up with electronic media that has exposed them to the best of the best in beauty, fashion, movies, music, transportation, homes, and food. You name it, they've either experienced it or seen it! They expect a presentation that is fast and well done. If it's not, it's outdated, and outdated equals irrelevant.

Of the two—excellence and authenticity—excellence is easier to achieve because it is visible and measurable. How? Take this example: The staff finally discards the "sacred junk" that gathers dust and piles up in every nook and cranny of the church. Stacks of long forgotten, unused hymnals disappear from the corners of the Sunday school rooms. They remove faded pictures of a Caucasian Jesus holding little lambs, and dingy walls receive a fresh coat of paint. They renovate and redecorate restrooms to look more like those at the local upscale restaurant than a neglected public facility. They replace bulletin boards and handwritten poster board signs with computer-generated images mounted on foamcore. They no longer use insider language in the bulletin, and anyone who walks in off the street can understand the format and wording. Leaders demonstrate commitment to their ministries by participating in training opportunities and initiating improvements. Servants demonstrate a paradigm shift from "close enough is good enough" to "whatever it takes." Excellence makes the water of the church exciting and attractive; it becomes a legitimate contender for the curious person's discretionary time when compared to the alternatives the world has to offer.

Authenticity is harder to achieve. It's invisible, and measured only by the feelings of others. The opposite of authentic is phony, and we all know what it feels like to be around someone who is phony, don't we? It leaves us cold. Authenticity, on the other hand, makes the water of the church feel warm and inviting.

I believe the lack of authenticity in our churches stems from buying into "the Myth of the Good Christian"[1]. It's the lie that says being a good Christian is about keeping the rules. Of course, no one actually knows what all the rules are. But all of us know there are way too many to keep. So, instead of actually keeping the rules, we *act* like we keep them. After all, if we let it be known that we really are nothing more than ordinary sinners, then we wouldn't look like good Christians, would we? And if we remove our masks and show who we really are, then somebody—maybe everybody—wouldn't like us. They might talk about us behind our backs, point fingers at us, and we would be humiliated. No! It's just too risky! And so the church becomes an incubator of inauthentic living.

While phony is the opposite of authentic, rule breaking is not the opposite of rule keeping. Jesus was labeled a rule breaker early in his ministry, but he addressed that issue in Matthew 5:17. *"Do not think that I have come to abolish the law or the Prophets; I have not come to abolish them but to fulfill them."* He wanted to make it clear that authentic living embraces both the letter of the law and the spirit of the law. In each section of the Sermon on the Mount, Jesus says, *"You have heard that it was said to the people long ago . . ."* referring to the Mosaic Law, the laws and practices of the Israelites. However, he emphasizes

[1]There is a myth that to be a "good' Christian you must follow the rules. No one can say what all the rules are, but some of those most commonly held are don't make waves, don't confront, don't tell others what to do, be happy, and say yes when asked to help, even if you really mean no.

that the law is not meant to isolate us from one another, but to pull us out of isolation into a deeper relationship with one another. Matthew 5:38-41 gives us an example:

> "You have heard that it was said, 'eye for eye, and tooth for tooth.' But I tell you, do not resist an evil person. If someone strikes you on the right cheek, turn to him the other also. And if someone wants to sue you and take your tunic, let him have your cloak as well. If someone forces you to go with him one mile, go with him two miles."

What Jesus is teaching is a way to live with others that differs from what was previously understood. The first way—"eye for eye and tooth for tooth"—is about keeping civil order. It is a system of justice that allowed the Israelite community to live together in civilized peace. It established that you are held responsible for your actions: if you injure, you will be injured; if you kill, you will be killed. But the different lifestyle Jesus teaches is a way that appeals to the heart and is motivated by love, not justice. He speaks of authentic caring that perseveres and proactively brings with it an undeniable and overwhelming love that suffocates the insults of the insulter and overrides the demands of the demander. He is not calling us to be doormats; he is calling us to be warrior-lovers, to both the churched and unchurched alike. This is the authenticity that will hold captive the life-seeking world that comes to the doors of our churches. When met by this kind of love-filled greeter, usher, or parking lot attendant, the world has no defense. People may squirm a little, walk away, or test to see if it is genuine, but, at the end of the day, they cannot deny their encounter with authentic love.

What Am I Going To Do about This?

When a curious, stage two, modern-day Nathaniel is met with hospitality that meets his expectation of excellence and is surprised by an encounter with a new acquaintance who is authentic, it confirms what his old trusted friend Philip said about the church back at the office. As he gets back in the car after worship and buckles his seatbelt, he faces a primary question. "That was surprisingly good." he thinks to himself. "What am I going to do about this?" This reaction is similar to Nathaniel's after encountering Jesus. "Then Nathaniel declared, 'Rabbi, you are the Son of God; you are the King of Israel!'"(John 1:49). In other words, "By golly! You *are* the real deal!"

Following a positive encounter, we begin to witness words and actions in this stage two person that are consistent with those of the Samaritans who came to the well. John 4:42 records it this way: *"They said to the woman, 'we no longer believe just because of what you said: now we have heard for ourselves, and we know that this man really is the Savior of the world."* In the case of both Nathaniel and the Samaritans, the invisible baton of trust had been passed from old trusted friends to the new acquaintance. Jesus had successfully received the handoff with the intentional care of an intimate warrior-lover. He spoke both truth and love into their cynical hearts, and was able to break down every barrier of resistance.

Last year, our senior pastor received a letter from a disgruntled stage two person who was testing the water at the church where I work. This man had made a decision to dip his toes in a little deeper and sign up for the church league softball team, thinking it would be a low commitment way to see if the church family was really as authentic as the pastor said it was. Arriving at the first practice, he encountered the team coach, who not only didn't play him, but also was quite obviously in it for the championship, not fellowship. The pastor's words from the pulpit did not match the actions of the softball coach, and when words and actions don't match, words are always the lie—or so it appeared to our second stage person. He had expected the authenticity he experienced in the lobby and from the mouth of the pastor, but what he found was counterfeit Christianity.

Our pastor forwarded the letter to me, asked me to check into the complaints, and address the situation. I watched and asked questions for several weeks, and by the end of the season, it was apparent that the man's complaints about our softball team were valid. The following spring, I initiated a total revamping of the sports ministry to make sure the primary emphasis was on Christian fellowship, not winning. Even though a year had passed since we received the letter, I decided to follow up with a phone call. I first checked the database to get a better idea of who I was about to call, and discovered that the man and his family had stopped attending our church shortly after he wrote the letter. My heart sank. I was angry with myself for waiting so long to call.

I gripped the receiver and dialed the number, hoping to reach an answering machine and not the man. Much to my surprise, he actually answered the phone in the middle of the afternoon! "Oh, boy!" I thought. "This fellows is going to let me have it." With sweaty palms, I proceeded to introduce myself and explained that I had the letter he wrote to the senior pastor the previous year. I apologized for the negative experience he had and told him that I spent a good deal of time checking out his complaints. I went on to thank him for bringing the issue to our attention and explained what had been done to revamp the sports ministry and correct the situation. Then I waited. There was silence on the other end of the line as I braced myself to be blasted and brushed off. What he said floored me. "You kept the letter?" he asked. "Yes," I replied. "Absolutely. I have it right here in my hand." The man said, "I thought that letter was long gone and my words had been forgotten. Mr. Glover, I am an ex-marine who coached national championship baseball teams while I was in the service. Over this past year, knowing my buddies are losing their lives overseas, I've begun to wonder what I was fighting for, until this conversation. Now I remember. I was fighting for this kind of truth. Mr. Glover, I will do everything in my power to be at church this coming Sunday. I want to meet you, sir, and if you would permit me, I would like to help coach the church's softball team this year." This time the silence was on my end of the phone. I was stunned and thrilled but managed to say, "Sure . . . I'd love to meet you!" And I meant it.

This man's encounter with our softball team had not been a good one. There were no new acquaintances to be found there. As a church that is committed to effective disciple making, we had to correct the problem and insure the coexistence of excellence and authenticity, even in our sports ministry. He wasn't looking for a theological explanation of salvation, or vast knowledge of the Bible. He simply needed those of us in the church to live out the authentic Christian life in front of him, so he could see that this really was a place where truth prevails. Those of us who are already in the water anxiously wait for the "water testers" to decide whether the temperature is warm or cold, and we delight in the wonder of it all when they say, "The water feels warm to me. I think I'll go for a swim!" With that decision, they step into stage three.

The primary components of stage two of the journey toward becoming a fully committed follower of Christ:

The primary person: Curious

The primary question: What am I going to do about this?

The primary relationship: New acquaintance

The primary barrier: Heightened sensitivity

The primary ministry: Authentic, high-impact hospitality

CHAPTER FOUR

Stage Three: Life in the Waves

I can't remember his name, but I think it was Ernie. He was a boy about my age, nine or ten years old, whom I met on one of our vacations to Nags Head. Ernie loved the ocean as much as I loved it. We met the first day we arrived, and I immediately forgot all about my sister. At last, I had someone who actually wanted to play in the water with me!

Our friendship started with a couple of glances, then he tossed a question my way. "Do you like to body surf?" he asked. That's all it took and away we went. Ernie became my best friend for the first four days of my vacation, and we didn't tire of each other for even a moment. We splashed in the ocean all day and searched for land crabs late into the evening. We introduced our parents to each other, and as a result our families even ate together. At the end of each day we dropped into bed unconscious for the night, then did it all again the next day. It was as if we stuffed a decade of relationship into that brief window of time.

That summer, Ernie and I enjoyed life to the fullest in waist deep water, and together we learned about the power of the ocean. We allowed the waves to pound our little boy heads into the sandy ocean floor, and then we jumped up, spitting seawater, and immediately searched for each other. When one would drift too far from shore, the other would shout, "Hey, get back here and play tag!" We instinctively knew we were no match for deep water, and we were content to stay in the shallows.

Something I truly appreciated about Ernie was that he never asked about the tee shirt my mom made me wear. Most kids would ask why I wore it in the water. Ocean, lake, pool . . . it didn't matter! Mom made me wear it, and I hated it. It was embarrassing, and I never had a very good answer except that she said so. In retrospect, I realize she was trying to protect my skin from exposure to too much sun. But Ernie never asked. He acted like he never noticed, and we played in the waves for hours.

Everything changed on the fourth day of what seemed like a perfect vacation. That day, a lesson from the deep drifted into our pristine world. Ernie and I were once again catching waves in our favorite spot of waist deep water. Our parents were on shore sunbathing, reading, talking, and keeping their eyes on us. Everything felt safe. Then I heard a little yelp from Ernie. It was the kind of quick startled cry you make when you step on something unexpected on the ocean floor and your whole body jumps straight up. It sounded so funny that I laughed as I spun around toward him. But, as I did, Ernie began to let out a blood-curdling scream and I froze in terror. Everything suddenly moved in slow motion, and my memories of the moments that followed are like an old movie reel slowly flipping through individual frames. Ernie had something wrapped around him and all four of our parents were running into the water toward us. I looked down at my tee shirt and what was wrapped around Ernie was wrapped around me as well. I felt the pain of something stinging me as my mother scooped me out of the water into her arms. Then someone yelled, "Man-of-war!" The tee shirt I hated so much kept me from most of the stinging tentacles of this floating mine field. Ernie wasn't so lucky. He had been much closer to the creature, and his legs and torso got caught up in the long, venomous strands of the jellyfish. The ambulance took Ernie away, and our perfect vacation was over.

After years of reflection on my summer vacation with Ernie, I realized there were life-lessons to be learned from the experiences we shared. I learned to respect the unpredictability of the ocean. I learned that the ocean is a different world than the one I came from, and it has rules of its own. I learned that I should not try to ignore those rules or I will not fare well. I also learned that the most important lessons about the awesome power of the ocean could be learned within twenty-five yards of the shoreline.

If we equate the first few yards of the ocean's surf to the first months and years following a person's entrance into the world of the church, we can begin to see how to prepare people for a deep and abiding relationship with God and the body of Christ. Ephesians 3:10 states, ". . . *through the church, the manifold wisdom of God will be made known."* While people are still in shallow, waist deep water, it is our responsibility to prepare and equip them to move toward the deep without being caught unaware.

A New or Rededicated Believer

A curious person experiencing the warm water of authentic encounters with new acquaintances and excellence in the church will decide to walk into the waist deep water of the third stage of development. The primary person at this stage is a new or rededicated believer.

A new believer is a person who gives his life to Christ for the first time. He or she may have previously brushed shoulders with the church in some minor fashion, such as a wedding or a funeral. He or she may even have attended a worship service from time to time, but by and large has not had a desire to connect in any meaningful way with a local church.

A rededicated believer is a person who previously waded into the deeper water of church life before he or she was fully equipped to do so, got cut off at the knees and became a dead body that washed back on shore. He or she has once again experienced the cynicism and heightened sensitivity of stages one and two, and is now moving slowly into the shallows to try it again.

It is important to understand the vulnerability of this person, and the sanctity of the act of rededication. Many will experience the emotion of being offended by a fellow believer at some point along the way. Each story is different, but the result is the same: emotional pain that makes returning to the church and facing the offender difficult. In fact, scripture describes this person in Proverbs 18:19. *"An offended brother is more unyielding than a fortified city, and disputes are like the barred gates of a citadel."* If not properly equipped to understand and interpret the incident, the offended party will emotionally shut down, bar the door, and allow no one to enter. It is the charge of every church leadership team to understand how to equip people *before* the attack happens, so as they move along the path of spiritual development, they will not only survive the challenges and risks, but also thrive in the exhilaration and beauty of the deep.

But let's get back to Ernie for a minute. I never saw him again, but my parents touched base with his parents and found out that he recovered and was doing fine. I was also told that Portuguese man-of-war don't usually drift that close to shore. We all know that larger more predatory sea creatures usually do not venture into shallow water. Only small life forms typically live there. Therefore, logic tells us that shallow water is safe for recreation. This simple principle is true in the church as well. Just as Ernie and I were too young and inexperienced to go into deep water, new and rededicated believers need to stay in the shallows while they become equipped to go deeper. Too often, we send a false message to people on the front end of their spiritual journeys that deep water is the only place of importance in the church. We unintentionally convey that the only stage of spiritual development that really matters is that of a fully committed follower. In doing so, we invite people who are not yet emotionally or spiritually equipped for the deep into water that is way over their heads. It looks like this: A person with years of experience as an executive is invited to become chairperson of the church leadership board. He obviously has the marketplace skills, but how spiritually developed is he? It never crosses our minds to take the time to check it out, does it? Many times this turns out to be someone who has no personal relationship with Christ, and therefore relates to people from a non-Christian worldview. It works in the marketplace! Won't it work in the church? (The ocean has rules of its own. If you ignore them, you will not fare well.) Conflict begins to brew, harsh words fly, and before you know it, another one bites the dust. There he goes, a dead body floating back to shore. He becomes disillusioned and cynical about the church, and the church complains about what a lousy job he did as board chairperson.

The Fork in the Road—How Can I Help? / How Can I Fit In?

The process of moving people into the deep too quickly begins innocently, and new or rededicated believers unwittingly contribute to the confusion when they ask the primary question at stage three. "How can I help?" they will ask with all the energy that comes from finally making the critical decision to get involved. The church, being powered by unpaid servants, is always on the lookout for talented women and men, but we who are in church leadership must exercise restraint. It is appealing to respond by moving these unspoiled, unequipped believers directly into service. Unfortunately, when we hear that question and take it at face value without taking into consideration the underlying meaning, when we put them directly into serving and overlook their deeper personal need, we drive a nail into the coffin of their spiritual development. Churches all across America do it every day, and then wonder why their people aren't maturing in their faith.

At first, they are energetic and full of ideas for the task they are performing. The honeymoon may last a year or more but, sooner or later, people begin to show signs of spiritual depravation. He doesn't show up for meetings and events as often as he once did. She begins to grumble about the church, maybe the leadership, or the direction the church is moving. Or, like Ernie and me, he may experience a painful encounter for which he is not emotionally or spiritually equipped. The result is the same. He gets cut off at the knees, becomes a dead body that washes ashore and stays on the beach until he either decides to try again or gives up and walks away from the church. To prevent the destruction that comes from moving new and rededicated believers directly into service as the primary means of connecting them to the life of the church, we must accurately interpret what they say, "How can I help?", and understand that what they mean is, "How can I fit in?"

What I am describing here are two differing philosophies. The first views serving as the road to spiritual maturity. The second views education and relationships that "equip the saints for service" as the pathway to transforming lives. *This is the fork in the road of intentional disciple making.* What your church does at this critical juncture will determine the depth to which your parishioners will mature. One way leads to a church filled with actively serving believers, while the other leads to a church filled with spiritually developed servants. As leaders charged with the advancement of God's kingdom, we must know and understand the invisible but very real difference between these two philosophies.

As we read these lines, very few will fess up and say, "Oh, yes! Our church drives nails into the spiritual growth coffins of new and rededicated believers all the time!" Therefore, to ascertain the truth, we must let our actions speak for themselves:

Of the last ten times you went to the church, not counting worship:

- How many times did you go to serve?

- How many times did you go to participate in a class, Bible study or support group?

Of the last ten church related phone calls you made:

- How many were for the sole purpose of talking about what God is doing in the life of the person you called?

- How many were to ask the person a task related question or recruit them to serve on a committee or team?

Of the last ten meetings you attended at the church:

- What percentage of each meeting was devoted to the task for which the group is responsible?

- What percentage was devoted solely to building relationships, leadership development, team building or spiritual growth?

In the last ten weeks:

- How many people have you spent time with talking about what has happened in your lives and what God is saying to each of you?

Here's the point. People do not come to church because they want or need ten more tasks to complete or ten more meetings to attend. And yet, a disconnected hodgepodge of activity and tasks is exactly what the church offers them in the belief that "getting involved" will somehow lead to the abundant life. We actually help people remain theologically uninformed and relationally isolated from one another, and all the while leave their spiritual lives to die on the vine.

There eventually comes a time when a person has assessed and determined that the focus of a church is on worship, fellowship, activities, and service, and discipleship is minimized. Each of these is an important component of the journey toward Christ-likeness, but when the internal issues of spiritual growth go unaddressed, there comes a dawning realization that no one is aware that those issues even exist. A person who finds him or herself in this church environment is left with only two options.

Option 1: Separation

Look at any collection of statistics and you will see that thousands of people have opted to separate from the church in the past fifty years. In the United States, the United Methodist denomination is divided into sixty-three annual conferences. Approximately five thousand people per year for each of the past fifteen years have stopped attending United Methodist churches in my conference alone![1]

Option 2: Conformity

It is impossible to track the number of people who conform to a church environment that does not help them develop spiritual muscle. Personal experience, however, has brought to my door both pastors and lay leaders who lament that their church is dead, their people are not growing, and the community around them is not being affected. These are the churches that are filled with people who conform and accept a non-transformational environment as the norm. Oh, they attend services and committee meetings, and they even show up for potluck dinners. But they have long since checked out mentally, emotionally, and—worst of all—spiritually. They assume they are a bit crazy for even entertaining the unspoken, internal questions that come when God begins whispering to them. The church isn't talking about it so they decide to figure it out on their own. And because there is no venue for spiritual encouragement, direction, guidance, or accountability, they choose the path of least resistance. Who would blame them

[1]West Ohio Conference Journals 1988-2003.

for avoiding risky faith steps that appear to fly in the face of common sense, and possibly cause hardship for their loved ones? What fault could be found with a man who chooses *not* to pursue his ministry calling because it would require his family to live with only the bare necessities for the next three years? It seems to make perfect sense that a wife and mother of two young children would give up a silly notion of starting a new ministry when her husband and children need her. It just seems right! Can you see how easy it is to choose conformity?

There is a mesmerizing effect at this stage of spiritual development. Like the tide, there is a constant rhythm to the day in, day out waves of church life. If we don't bother to discover our life purpose, there will still be a worship service on Sunday. If we don't follow God's voice that we hear late at night when the noise of the day subsides, Bible study will still roll around on Wednesday night. We may know God wants us to launch a soup kitchen, but if we don't take that faith step, surely someone else will. There will always be another trustees' meeting, and the monthly newsletter will always arrive the second week of the month. We will sing the same familiar hymns, and there will be an ice cream social in August. And the comfortable, predictable rhythm of church life slowly rocks us into spiritual slumber. When we choose the path of conformity, any idea of following God into the deep, risky places God longs to take us seems so unnecessary. There's so much to do at the church right now, why bother?

Giving and Receiving

But there is a fire that burns within us. It's an eternal flame that was lit by God at our birth. We do our best to deny it, medicate it, modify it, and downplay it. *Anything* but pursue it! But it just won't go away. Occasionally, the flame briefly flickers brighter when someone takes an extra close look, catches a glimpse of it, and speaks to us of what they saw. When that happens, we become energized and don't understand why. The energy surges through us because we have brushed close to the kingdom of God that has been placed inside us, and for just a moment, it has been revealed. Ecclesiastes 3:11 puts it this way, *"He has also set eternity in the hearts of men; yet they cannot fathom what God has done from beginning to end."* The way the fire is stoked and eternity is awakened in our hearts is not through separation that moves us out of the church altogether, or from one church into another. It is not through conformity to the mesmerizing rhythm of church life. It is through the two components of the primary ministry to a stage three person, a giving and receiving ministry. The first component is relevant and practical instruction that mentally, emotionally, and spiritually equips us for what lies ahead. The second component is bold, authentic, God-listening, life-giving relationships with other Christians.

Instruction

Prior to our encounter with the man-of-war, Ernie and I thought we were masters of our universe. That distorted view was based on our immaturity and what little we had learned in the few feet of water into which we had ventured. In retrospect, the man-of-war actually served us well by instilling a sober respect for the dangers that were just beyond our sight in deeper water.

To thrive or even survive in the deep, Ernie and I would have required far more training than we had. While this is obvious to anyone considering an ocean adventure, it is not as obvious in relation to our spiritual lives. When we parallel the spiritual journey toward a deeper relationship with God to a journey into the deep and powerful ocean, we can see that no amount of preparation will ever fully equip us for the totality of what God has in store. But, through adequate preparation, we can see and experience far more than is possible without it. By preparation I mean developing a more accurate view of God and ourselves, and applying what we learn on a daily basis. The church must be intentional in selecting the classes and groups it offers to effectively equip believers for their journeys toward becoming fully committed followers of Christ.

There are three areas of instructional emphasis that will help equip stage three travelers for the rest of the journey:

Spiritual disciplines—how to study the Bible, meditate on scripture and keep a journal, private and corporate worship, tithing, etc.

Theology—an understanding of the true nature of God, the basic beliefs of the Christian faith, the characteristics of a fully committed follower of Jesus, the fundamental truths of the Bible, etc.

Practical application of scripture—how to cultivate a Christ-centered marriage, how to raise godly children, what scripture has to say about money management and how to apply those principles, how to overcome destructive behaviors, how to recover from personal crisis, etc.

When I hear someone lament the wrong they experienced at the hand of another Christian, it often is the result of venturing too far into deeper water without adequate advance instruction that would have equipped them for the experience. Every Bible verse we read, every class we take, every journal entry we make, will become a valuable and beneficial tool in times of darkness.

Let me be clear about the nature of instruction as a component of an effective giving and receiving ministry. Instruction is not about merely transferring information. It is about transforming others by renewing their minds and developing a Christian worldview that resists the pull of the culture in every area of life. The education committees and departments of our churches must strive to offer curriculum that is relevant to the people in our culture, and present it in a relational setting that provides opportunities for interaction and creates hungry learners. The church leadership must intentionally develop a culture of learning by conveying the benefits of greater knowledge and understanding. When new or rededicated believers ask the question, "How can I help?" and we accurately interpret the underlying question, "How can I fit in?", we are able to direct them to classes and groups that prepare them for the spiritual journey ahead. This is how the church stops contributing to the number of dead bodies that wash ashore as a result of being ill equipped for the Christian life.

Authentic Relationships

The primary relationships needed to help move a stage three person forward are effective preachers, teachers, and small group leaders. Effective preachers and teachers have the gift of agitation. That's what a preacher or teacher is supposed to do: create internal spiritual agitation that stokes the fire within. They cause us to contemplate and internally wrestle with spiritual issues. But they are only part of the equation. Week after week, many of us walk away from a powerful sermon or thought provoking Bible study and feel as if we've just had our spiritual clocks cleaned. Unfortunately, we have nowhere to work through the agitation that was appropriately created in us. This is where an effective small group leader comes into play, by addressing the spiritual agitation they observe in us, providing a trust-filled environment where we can safely confess our God-dreams, and fanning the flame that burns inside us.

The combination of agitation from a distance by preachers and teachers and agitation up close in face-to-face small group encounters is demonstrated in Luke 5:3-6:

> "He (Jesus) got into one of the boats, the one belonging to Simon, and asked him to put out a little from the shore. Then he sat down and taught the people from the boat. When he had finished speaking, he said to Simon, 'Put out into deep water and let down your nets for a catch.' Simon answered, 'Master, we've worked hard all night and haven't caught anything. But, because you say so, I will let down the nets.' When they had done so, they caught such a large number of fish that their nets began to break."

Jesus taught from a distance as he sat in Simon's boat. The distance allows a person in the crowd to receive the truth of a message and not be put on the spot to respond. He or she is able to hear and digest it. An emotional cord will be momentarily struck in some, but leave no lasting impression. Others will be lost in thought about personal matters and not hear a word of the message. Others, however, will be pierced by the message, the flame will be stoked, and the agitation will begin.

The work of an effective preacher or teacher is to emotionally move and spiritually challenge us to become the men and women God created us to be. To be effective, their messages and lessons must come from deep within, and be delivered with excellence, passion, and conviction that reflects their understanding of the topic. They spend themselves on behalf of a message that makes scriptural truth come alive with relevance and meaning. However, these sermons and lessons are not the end all of spiritual development for the women and men in our congregations. They are the front-end fire-starters that must be followed by face-to-face interaction that fans the flame, provides a place to process the accompanying agitation, and break through with new insights.

Comfort

After teaching the crowd, Jesus turned face-to-face to Simon and personally invited him to put out into deep water. Jesus understood that the fuller possibilities of what truth reveals could only be realized through deeper relational interaction. Look at Simon's response in verse 5a: *"Master, we've worked hard all night and haven't caught anything."* In other words, Simon said, "We've already done that. It didn't work before and it probably won't work now." When confronted by his effective small group leader, Simon articulated the primary barrier at stage three—comfort.

The same rhythm of church life that can lull us into spiritual slumber and conformity also causes us to resist the deep. We subtly convince ourselves that we have experienced everything there is to the Christian life. Been there, done that! Why should we inconvenience ourselves by casting off from shore and letting our nets down again? We already know what will happen, don't we?

The real danger of the comfort barrier is that we underestimate its power. We don't actually believe we are held captive by it. When challenged to get out of our comfort zones, we say, "No problem!" But when its time to act on those words, we can't quite seem to follow through. In Andrei Konchalovsky's film adaptation of Homer's epic poem, *The Odyssey*, Odysseus' ship is blown off course and he and his men find themselves on the island of Aeaea. Circe, the goddess who resides there, gives them a potion that erases from their memories any thoughts of home, their ultimate destination. His men fall under the spell, but Odysseus, who has consumed an herb to protect himself from the effects of the drink, does not. Circe releases the men from the magical charm after striking a deal with Odysseus. However, he and his men choose to remain and indulge in the pleasures offered by their hostess. The day eventually comes when Odysseus announces to Circe that he and his men must resume their journey to their beloved homeland after enjoying her company for the previous five days. Circe laughs at his lack of understanding that he had not been on the island for five days but for five years! Stunned, Odysseus runs to the beach only to find his ship nearly covered by five years of shifting sand. He and his men had set aside their journey and allowed themselves to be sidetracked by giving in to the mesmerizing comfort of their surroundings. Like Odysseus, we can easily be lulled into the invisible grip of comfort and wile away our days, until we suddenly realize that we have remained in the safety of the shallows, never moving forward, most of our lives.

In Luke 5:5b, you can see what breaks the powerful pull of comfort and convenience in Simon's life. Although he stated his opposition to Jesus' request to drop the fishing nets again, he goes on to say,

"But because you say so, I will let down the nets." The disciples had a high degree of respect for Jesus' authority. They did as he asked, no matter how illogical it seemed, because they trusted him. It is in this type of trust relationship that the strength of a small group leader is found. Small group leaders are able to get close enough to find out who we really are. If we respect and trust them, God can use that relationship to draw us into the deep water, where our nets can catch the full measure of what God intends for us.

The value of authentic relationships is revealed in the interaction between Paul and the church at Philippi. Philippians 4:14-15 says, *"Yet it was good of you to share in my troubles. Moreover, as you Philippians know, in your early acquaintance with the gospel, when I set out from Macedonia, not one church shared with me in this matter of giving and receiving except you only."* Paul is arguably the greatest missionary the world has ever seen. The stories of his fearlessness in the book of Acts and his subsequent letters are nothing short of legendary. It would be easy to categorize Paul as a one-of-a-kind man who needed no help navigating the risky, deep water of God's calling. But his words indicate that the elders at the Philippian church had won the heart of this warrior-evangelist.

"Yet it was good of you to share in my troubles." Paul was never a man to put his own needs on the table. He only recounted his personal difficulties when making a point to win others to the gospel of Christ. However, this statement is entirely different, and is one of a man thanking a group of fellow believers from the bottom of his heart. This is the statement of a man remembering that he had been offered not only a platform for his message but also a place of personal, empowering interaction.

"Moreover, as you Philippians know in your early acquaintance with the gospel when I set out from Macedonia . . ." This personal interaction began right away. I believe it is revealed in the encounter he had with Lydia as recorded in Acts 16:11-15. It was the Sabbath, and Paul and his group were outside the city gate when he began to speak to the women gathered there. Verses 14b and 15 record the moment the Lord opened the heart of Lydia: *"The Lord opened her heart to respond to Paul's message. When she and the members of her household were baptized, she invited us to her home. 'If you consider me a believer in the Lord,' she said, 'come and stay at my house.' And she persuaded us."* This was the beginning of the relationship Paul had with the Philippian church. It was obviously not merely about Paul preaching and doing the work of an evangelist. The people were moved to listen to the message, open their homes, and extend themselves for Paul and his men. They cared for them on a personal level.

". . . not one church shared with me in this matter of giving and receiving, except you only." Finally, Paul names the difference between this church and every other church he encountered. They had filled his empty cup, so to speak. They had entered into a relationship where each gave and each received. It was not one-dimensional.

This passage gives us great insight into the relational component of spiritual need. It is not satisfied through the completion of a task alone. Although many make their first connection into the life of the church by serving, they will go unfulfilled until someone moves beyond what they produce and extends an invitation, as Lydia did to Paul, to receive something. Suddenly, Paul was not the giver, but the receiver. He acknowledged in this verse that the Philippian church was the one and only church that looked beyond his service and was concerned about him as a person. They demonstrated this concern for his personal, unspoken needs by proactively and intentionally giving back to him. They took time to see the man, not just the traveling church planter. In doing so, they won his heart, showed him love in practical ways, and provided the invisible fortification needed to survive in the deep.

There is good reason to remain at this third stage of spiritual development for a while. It is a safe place where time should be devoted to broadening our understanding of ourselves, the nature of God, and the development of trusting relationships. It is a time to establish a pattern of internal spiritual analysis that reflects the Psalmist words from Psalm 139:23-24: *"Search me, O God and know my heart; test me and know my anxious thoughts. See, if there is any offensive way in me, and lead me in the way everlasting."* Only a prepared heart will allow us to survive the vastness and risks of the open water. People who have not spent adequate time at this stage and venture into deeper places of influence and leadership in the church typically become causalities or create spiritual chaos. New and rededicated believers must use this time in the swallows wisely. It is a place where God, through relationships and careful instruction, searches our hearts, tests our thoughts, and looks for any offensive ways in us before calling us into deeper water. The church must create comfort for those in stages one and two, but not allow it to become the barrier for those at stage three. We must encourage stage three travelers to go further and continue seeking God's purpose for their lives in stage four.

The primary components of stage three of the journey toward becoming a fully committed follower of Christ:

The primary person: New or rededicated believer
The primary question: How can I help?
The underlying question: How can I fit in?
The primary relationship: Effective preachers, teachers, and small group leaders
The primary barrier: Comfort
The primary ministry: Giving and receiving

CHAPTER FIVE

Stage Four: Life When Your Feet Come Off the Bottom

Gary and Debbie were part of a small group with my wife and me in the late 1990s, and were excited about taking a family vacation to the Hawaiian Islands. Upon arrival, they were greeted by warm sun and lush scenery surrounded by the sparkling sea. Everything seemed perfect, but we received a phone call from Debbie after only five days. They were cutting their trip short and returning to Ohio immediately. Gary had been involved in a freak accident that nearly cost him his life, and to make matters worse, he had suffered a minor stroke. They would soon be home and promised to fill us in on the details. Gary was given center stage to share the story of his horrifying experience when our small group next met. Still visibly shaken, he described his close encounter with a riptide that nearly washed him out to sea.

On this particular day, Gary, Debbie, and their three children decided to spend the day enjoying the warm waters of the Pacific. After driving past many beaches, they came to a beautiful stretch of sand along the north shore. It was a small beach, with fingers of land jutting out into the water on either side creating a peaceful, secluded cove. It appeared to be an ideal tropical hideaway. They unpacked the car and settled in on the beach for a day of family fun.

One of their daughters was the first one in the water with Gary right behind her. They were having a wonderful time splashing in the surf, when Gary noticed the currents make a sudden shift. Feeling a strong flow of water tugging at his legs, he yelled to his daughter to begin swimming toward shore, but their attempts to get back to the beach seemed fruitless. No matter how hard they stroked they seemed to make no headway. What they had not anticipated as they stepped into the water of this seemingly tranquil cove was a riptide, a narrow, jet-like stream of water that flows out to sea in a direction perpendicular to a beach. Both Gary and his daughter were caught in the powerful stream of water that was rushing out to sea, and didn't know how to escape.

From the beach, Debbie heard Gary shout and could see that he and their daughter were both struggling. She raced into the water to help, not realizing what was happening below the surface. When she was no more than knee deep, however, the towel she carried was sucked right out of her hand by the rushing undercurrent. She knew she had to turn back, or find herself pulled into the deep water of the ocean as well. All she could do was scream to her husband and daughter to swim harder!

After nearly twenty minutes of intense struggle, Gary and his daughter both reached the shallows. Debbie dragged them ashore, but soon after Gary suffered a minor stroke from the massive effort he had exerted. Gary and his family clearly had not been prepared for the deep water in which they found themselves.

When we describe the fourth stage of spiritual development in workshops around the country, we ask the audience if they can remember a time when they swam in the ocean and their feet came off the bottom. we ask them to think back to their attempt to find solid footing, but when they reached down for the bottom, there was nothing there. "Remember," we ask. "when you reached down a second time and there *really* was nothing there? What does every fiber in your body tell you to do at that moment?" The entire room invariably will shout in response, *"Go back to the beach!"*

We typically do not see the need to be equipped to face the dangers of deep water when we go to the ocean to play and splash close to shore. When we find ourselves drifting too far from shallow water, our natural response is to move back in toward a safer, more comfortable depth. Our spiritual lives are the same. We enter into the life of the church and give ourselves over to a personal relationship with Christ. We are new creations, and in those early days we feel as though the experience is all about "me and my spiritual growth." We spiritually splash around in the shallows, gain a better understanding of our new environment, and build relationships with others who are in the water with us. We stay at a safe and comfortable depth, and gradually get into the rhythm of church life. This wave action carries with it an underlying riptide that can easily pull an unprepared person too quickly into water that is over his or her head. Eventually, we begin to feel the tug toward deeper water. We entertain new thoughts as God begins calling to us to take a risk and join God in a deep, abiding relationship. We begin to realize there is a bigger, more expansive reason for this relationship with Christ, and feel God trying to move us to an unfamiliar place that is the fourth stage of spiritual development. If adequately equipped, stage four becomes an exhilarating adventure. For those ill prepared to navigate the shift in current, like Gary, it can become an experience that leaves a person paralyzed.

The Seasoned But Restless Believer

The primary person at this stage of spiritual development is the seasoned but restless believer. This person has left behind his or her heightened sensitivity, and is thoroughly comfortable with his or her surroundings, beliefs, circle of friends and acquaintances. There is not too much in church life that surprises this person anymore. Having taken all the classes, worked through various ministry positions, and attended all the events, he or she understands the church family and the Christian life, and it feels like home.

However, the internal restlessness will not go away. It's not the same as the agitation of stage three that is the result of the Holy Spirit convicting us through an effective preacher, teacher, or small group leader. This is different. This feels like frustration or anxiety, but it's not. It's a nagging sense that life is not complete, not quite what it should be, there's more. It sometimes manifests itself as a complacent attitude toward things we once found energizing or fulfilling, such as Bible studies or worship. It may sound like frustration, aggravation, or complaint about how the church does ministry. How long this season of restlessness lasts varies from person to person. For those who are receptive to and seek out wise counsel and interpretation, the time-frame can be relatively short. For those who have no one to accurately interpret the restlessness or are not receptive to wise counsel, the restlessness could go on indefinitely. In the latter case, separation from the church may result in an effort to feel comfortable again.

But feeling comfortable is not the issue. The traveler must have a solid understanding of how God grows disciples because, in stage four, the traveler must make a conscious choice to move beyond this point or not. The traveler can emotionally react to his or her uncomfortable feelings, or draw from the skill and wisdom acquired in stage three. If the traveler spent his or her preparation time in shallow relationships and resisting or avoiding biblical instruction, he or she will either choose to stay and not move forward to fulfill his or her purpose, or rush ahead unable to overcome the obstacles that arise. Following his near-fatal encounter with the riptide, Gary learned that he reacted out of fear and not out of skill and wisdom that should have been acquired in advance. To overcome the pull of a riptide, a person must allow the current to draw him into deeper water while swimming to one side or the other. There are currents at either side that draw water back to the shore at the same time the riptide draws water out into the ocean. The side currents actually carry a person back to safety. To accomplish this, however, one must overcome the fear of being drawn into deeper water. Feeling comfortable is not the issue.

Is There Anything Else?

The primary question on the mind of the seasoned but restless believer is this: "Is there anything else?" Has the believer really heard it all and seen it all, or is there something more to this Christian life? The restlessness comes from a yearning for the something more he or she knows is out there, just beyond reach. The words of Solomon in Ecclesiastes 2:1-3 serve to offer a glimpse at the searching heart of a person at this stage:

> "I thought in my heart, 'Come now, I will test you with pleasure to find out what is good.' But that also proved to be meaningless. 'Laughter,' I said, 'is foolish and what does pleasure accomplish?' I tried cheering myself with wine, and embracing folly—my mind still guiding me with wisdom. I wanted to see what was worthwhile for men to do under heaven during the few days of their life."

Solomon had equipped himself with all the world had to offer only to find himself at an intersection where everything seemed *"meaningless, a chasing after the wind."* His restless heart told him there was something more.

Solomon reflects the change that is taking place inside the stage four person in verse 3. *"I wanted to see what was worthwhile . . . "* Stage four is a time of pondering, a time of testing every thought and truth. Once again, believers feel lost. To this point, the spiritual journey has been all about them. Now, they are in transition toward a transformation that will bring with it an understanding that it's not about them at all, and they feel lost and confused. They can stop the confusion by giving up their search for something more worthwhile, to use Solomon's term. But, if they continue the search, they will continue to move into unfamiliar territory . . . and that's when their feet come off the bottom.

Three Faces of Fear

In those moments when we realize we have drifted out past the familiar feel of sand under our feet, we come face to face with the primary barrier to forward movement for the stage four traveler: fear. A very formidable barrier on its own, fear becomes even more powerful when coupled with the comfort of stage three that constantly pulls us back toward familiar shallows. In stage four, we repeatedly face the choice of moving forward into an unknown future or going back into a predictable past.

Through informal surveys we have conducted in workshops over the past ten years, it appears that 90 to 95% of regular church attendees are somewhere between stages three and four of spiritual development. They hear from the pulpit, Christian authors, and television and radio preachers that deeper faith and commitment is what Christianity is all about. None of us consciously want to remain shallow in our faith, so we don't resist the idea of life at a deeper level. But life in deeper water is not the same as life in more shallow water, and there are many obstacles to face. Following God into transformational places demands harder work, more time, and greater inconvenience. At stage three, life was comfortable, things seemed to fall into place, and it was easy to see God at work. The reassuring confirmations that came easily when we made choices are fewer and less clear in stage four. As the demands of greater commitment and deeper relationship increase, it's easy to think, "I must have made a wrong turn. This can't be what God intends for me. This is too hard." Do not underestimate the ability of these obstacles to bring progress toward a deeper, more abiding relationship with God to a halt. Emotional comfort is often a top priority, and many people are not willing to make the sacrifice of time, effort, and convenience.

As formidable as these comfort-based obstacles may be, they pale in comparison to the powerful intimidation of fear that manifests itself in three ways. The first invisible facet of fear encountered as we seek deeper places in our relationship with God is confusion. We have a longing for greater meaning and begin asking, "Is there anything else?" The questions we ask ourselves and others become tougher. The restlessness increases. The world doesn't look or feel right. Nothing calms the agitation inside. We become confused and ask ourselves and God, "What is this, and why is it happening to me?" As we search for answers, we can easily become convinced that we have stepped out of God's will, and the proper course of action is to pull up anchor and mentally move back to a place of comfort, back to the shallows where things are much more predictable. But confusion always accompanies a journey into the unknown. We simply cannot be familiar with a place we've never been until we get there. Confusion will cease when the journey moves us to the destination God has for us, so perseverance and proper interpretation of the confusion is critical at this stage.

The second invisible facet of fear is the questioning of our own value. As we submit and allow God to move us forward, confusion begins to diminish and we catch a glimpse of what God has in store. Typically, the enormity of what God intends for us is so overwhelming that we gasp for breath and immediately question our ability to accomplish God's work. "I can't do that! There's no way!" we cry. We find ourselves in good company when we doubt our ability to fulfill God's purpose for our lives. God said to Moses at the burning bush, *"I have indeed seen the misery of my people in Egypt . . . so I have come to rescue them from the hand of the Egyptians . . . so now, go. I am sending you to Pharaoh to bring my people the Israelites out of Egypt"* (Exodus 3). Stunned, Moses said, *"Who am I?"* Just as we do, Moses looked at himself, a mere shepherd from Midian, and immediately questioned his value in God's plan. His fear was based on who he saw himself to be at that moment, without understanding that God was speaking to the transformed Moses he was yet to become. It is to the men and women we are yet to become through God's transforming power that God reveals a glimpse of the plan for our lives.

In Judges 6:12, the angel of the Lord sat down next to Gideon and spoke to him as the man into which God was transforming him. *"'The Lord is with you, mighty warrior.'" 'But sir,' Gideon replied, 'if the Lord is with us?'"* Notice that the angel did not say, "The Lord is with *us* . . ." The angel said, "The Lord is with *you* . . . " Nevertheless, Gideon did what so many of us do when things get uncomfortably personal. He tried to deflect the individual nature of God's call back to a more generalized understanding. We are all comfortable with the fact that God loves and cares for the poor and needy, but when God tells us that we are the answer to the poor and needy in our part of the world, we begin to squirm. We can't see how it is possible, and we question our worth and ability to do what God asks. In verse 15, we see Gideon's full-blown attempt to convince the Lord of his inability to accomplish the work. His objection is based, like Moses, on how he viewed himself at that moment. *"'But Lord,' Gideon asked, 'How can I save Israel? My clan is the weakest in Manasseh, and I am the least in my family.'"* In the case of both Moses and Gideon, God's answer is clear. For Moses, God stated in Exodus 3:12, *"I will be with you."* For Gideon in Judges 6:16, God said, *"I will be with you."* I don't know about you, but I think I see a pattern. Proper interpretation of God's vision for us, combined with the understanding of ourselves and the nature of God that we developed in stage three, pays off here when we remember that God will not leave us or forsake us, that God will never give us more than we can endure, and that faith is being sure of what we do not see.

The third invisible facet of fear is a lack of direction. Once we submit to God and allow God to move us forward through the confusion, remembering that the vision of what God has is store is possible through Christ who strengthens us, we find ourselves at a loss for what steps to take next. We think, "I don't have a clue how to make this happen!" and the fear of failure begins to well up inside us. As scripture shows, God had little concern that Moses and Gideon had no clue what to do next. Instead, God promised to be with them at all times and serve as their guide. In the New Testament, Jesus served as a guide in the flesh for the disciples. He said to Simon Peter and Andrew, *"'Come follow me, and I will make you fishers of men'"* (Matthew 4:19). Jesus called to James and John *"and immediately they left the boat and their father and followed him"* (Matthew 4:21-22). Matthew 9:9 says, *"As Jesus went on from there he saw a man named Matthew sitting at a tax collector's booth. 'Follow me', he told him, and Matthew got up and followed him."* And John 1:43 says, *"The next day Jesus decided to leave for Galilee. Finding Philip he said to him, 'Follow me.'"* None of these men, from Moses to Philip, were expected to figure it out alone. The disciples were invited to join the Rabbi, and they followed so closely that they were covered with the dust kicked up by him along the way. Each one was instructed how to get the job done, and every question that crossed their minds was adequately answered. That is not to say their faith went untested and hardships were not encountered. It simply means that those who accept God's challenge to move toward their purpose do not have to know the answers in advance.

The church, however, has not done its job when it comes to discipling stage four believers as they seek to discover their purpose. The Christian community most often reacts inappropriately to the frustration seen in restless believers, instead of carefully watching, listening, and discerning. A growing discontent develops as God draws stage four believers further into the deep. They look at their church-related experiences and misinterpret the agitation. With only previous faith experiences to draw on, they look outward for the cause of their agitation. They say things like, "I can't do this ministry anymore! It's just too much!" "I'm not being fed. Aren't there any classes with more 'meat"? "I don't know why, but worship just doesn't do it for me anymore. Can't we be more spiritual?" These are the people we confuse with and discount as complainers because they demonstrate behavior we consider unbecoming a "good" Christian. We feel more comfortable when they are stuffed back into the old familiar boxes from which they came, but they won't have any part of it. It's easy to misinterpret spiritual restlessness and label it anger or mid-life crisis, but an honest search for what more life has to offer is always accompanied by restlessness, and we as church leaders must learn to identify authentic stage four restless believers, differentiate them from the chronic complainers who gripe about most everything, and help them move forward in their journey toward becoming fully committed followers of Christ.

We must also guard against taking the opposite approach with restless believers. When those who have seen a vision of God's plan for them finally muster the courage to step forward and confess their dreams, the church must be intentional about walking with them, instead of sending them out with our blessing to develop and implement ministry. We must remember that God calling them out and transforming them into mighty warriors, but they are not ready to accomplish God's will on their own until they are properly equipped.

The Small Group Leader and the Emerging Discipler

The primary relationships that help properly interpret the obstacles and barriers at stage four and offer appropriate direction and guidance are the small group leader and the emerging discipler. Seasoned but restless stage four believers long for women and men who have gone ahead of them into deeper water, and who will listen and help them interpret the restlessness, confusion and fear that is churning inside them. Listen to Jesus' words to the disciples in the upper room. *"The words I say to you are not just my own. Rather, it is the Father, living in me, who is doing his work"* (John 14:10). He goes on to say, *"Remain in me, and I will remain in you"* (John 15:9). *"As the Father has loved me, so have I loved you. Now remain in my love"* (John 16:1). *"All this I have told you so that you will not go astray"* (John 16: 31-32). *"'You believe at last,' Jesus answered. 'But a time is coming, and has come, when you will be scattered, each to his own home. You will leave me all alone'"* (John 16: 31-32). What Jesus is saying to the disciples is this, "You are moving into deep water, and sometimes you will find yourself in way over your head. I have relied on the Father to take me places I couldn't go alone and you can rely on me. Take to heart the message I share with you, because to do otherwise will not establish the fortitude required to succeed. Only the lessons learned from relationships where hearts have entwined in the pursuit of truth will endure through the hardships that lay ahead." These are not the words of a casual friend or one who merely transfers information. These are the words of a person who shares life transformation, and it is the model of a discipler and an effective small group leader. A discipler loves his disciples and blends fierce loyalty to the truth with great expectation of who his disciple can become.

A small group leader must always strive to be a discipler, but not all disciplers are small group leaders. The discipler may be a church elder, staff person, or ministry leader. Whether the stage four person turns to his or her small group leader to interpret the internal restlessness or to a discipler outside the small group is of no consequence. What does matter is that the discipler understands how to serve as an instrument of God's transforming power in the life of another.

Disciplers and effective small group leaders employ five relational tools in their interaction with others. They have learned to wait for trust to develop in their relationships and not become overly zealous in their efforts to disciple another. At the same time, they have developed the courage to ask the tough questions because they value the truth of God more than they value being liked by the one they disciple. If we as church leaders fall prey to the Myth of the Good Christian[1], we will not recognize the effective disciplers in our midst and promote a watered down version of disciple making that produces nothing more than believers who never take the plunge into deep water.

The five tools of a disciple maker are progressive and used in sequence. The discipler takes an intentional action step using the first tool, and the disciple reacts in a predictable manner that leads to the use of the next tool, and so on. The first tool is encouragement that is authentic, not counterfeit. Authentic encouragement causes the disciple to recognize that the discipler genuinely values and respects him or her as a person. Counterfeit encouragement, on the other hand, is at best a polite verbal pat on the back that carries with it no genuine concern for another. Jesus implored his followers to understand the difference by offering illustrations of the Good Samaritan, who defied socially acceptable patterns of behavior and came to the aid of the beaten man, of turning the other cheek, of going the second mile, of giving up a cloak as well as a tunic, and explanations of who our neighbors really are. Authentic encouragement builds trust, and once trust is built, the disciple finds the courage to confess his her restlessness and dreams to the discipler.

---

[1] "Good" Christians don't make waves, don't confront, don't tell others what to do, are happy, and say yes when asked to help even if they really mean no.

The second tool is the ability to receive and respond appropriately to the personal self-disclosure of another. An effective discipler will receive whatever the disciple has to say without judgment and, together, they launch into a healthy exploration of who the disciple is today, what God is nudging that person to do with his or her life, and how to move forward toward that future.

Subsequent conversations employ tool number three. The third tool used by an effective disciple maker is the ability to offer direction and guidance that is relevant and consistent with biblical truth. The restless believer facing the fear barrier typically does not know the next steps to take, and becomes paralyzed in his or her ability to move forward. He or she needs a discipler to accurately interpret the situation and offer guidance in four major life areas. The disciple's willingness to address issues surrounding these areas determines whether or not he or she can move forward. These major life areas are:

Personal and family issues—the day in and day routines of life and the people with whom they live

Ministry—the God-ordained purpose for which they were placed on this earth

Spiritual disciplines—the practices that teach them how to recognize God

Destructive behaviors—actions and patterns in their lives that run contrary to a Godly existence.

Jesus demonstrated how to offer direction and guidance in his relationship with the disciples. He showed them how he approached difficulty, how he overcame storms, and how he viewed and accepted death. He talked with them about how to live godly lives by living it out in front of them and addressing their questions along the way.

Tool number four is accountability—the practice of taking another person's life seriously enough to hold him or her responsible for developing the biblical lifestyle that person says he or she wants. Accountability is not condemning or critical. It's simply keeping in front of the disciple that which the person confessed as the desire of his or her heart. The discipler has offered biblical direction and guidance, and the only thing left to do is take the next step. An effective discipler expects the disciple to take it. After listening to the confessions and heart-felt desires of so many, Jesus would often simply tell them to do it. He said to the paralytic, *"Rise, pick up your mat and walk"* (Mark 2:11). When Peter saw Jesus walking on the water, he stood up in the boat and said, *"If it is you . . . tell me to come to you and I will be able to." Jesus replied, "Come"* (Matthew 14:28-29). Like Jesus, effective disciplers take people seriously enough to hold them responsible for the confessed desires of their hearts.

The fifth tool is loving confrontation. There comes a time when discipling relationships risk friendship in favor of the biblical truth. This is the moment when the relationship has the potential to become an enduring alliance between two people who forfeit their pride in search of godly lives. When truth wins out, the disciple and the discipler can become an unstoppable force for the kingdom. This is the heart of Jesus' statement in Matthew 18:19 when he says to the disciples, *"Again, I tell you that if two of you on earth agree about anything you ask for, it will be done for you by my Father in heaven."* In this passage he is giving the disciples a glimpse of the power God places in the hands of two who have confronted the truth and moved together in obedience to the new reality that has been revealed. In Mark 10:17-22, the rich young ruler approaches Jesus and confesses the desire of his heart. *"As Jesus started on his way, a man ran up to him and fell on his knees before him. 'Good teacher, he asked, what must I do to inherit eternal life?' 'You know the commandments: Do not murder, do not commit adultery, do not steal, do not give false testimony, do not defraud, honor your father and mother.'"* He came to worship every Sunday, had taken all the classes, worked his way through various ministry positions, and attended all the events. He understood church life and it felt like home, except for the internal restlessness that would not go away. He was looking for more. *"'Teacher,' he declared, 'all these I have kept since I was a boy.' Jesus looked at the man and loved him. 'One thing you lack,' he said, 'Go, sell everything you have and give to the poor, and you will have treasure in heaven. Then come follow me.'"* An effective discipler confronts disciples and continues to love them in spite of the choice they make to either move forward into the deep or return to the safety of shallow water. The bible tells of the man's response to his moment of truth. *"At this the man's face fell. He went away sad, because he had great wealth."* Of course, not all turn away. Those who choose to act on the truth and move ahead have the adventure of a lifetime in store.

Go and See

It is within the context of this type of biblically based discipling relationship that the primary ministry to a stage four believer begins to emerge. Scripture identifies it in the midst of the story of the feeding of the 5,000 as told in Mark 6:35-38. *"By this time it was late in the day, so his disciples came to him. 'This is a remote place,' they said, 'and its already very late. Send the people away so they can go to the surrounding countryside and villages and buy themselves something to eat.' But he answered, 'You give them something to eat.' They said to him, 'That would take eight months of a man's wages! Are we to go and spend that much on bread and give it to them to eat?' 'How many loaves do you have?' he asked, 'Go and see.'"* The primary ministry in stage four is opportunities to go and see. Seasoned but restless believers who are searching for more need opportunities to go and see what they are capable of doing as they uncover the purpose for which God created them.

Jesus was thoroughly established as the leader of this group of men. He was the teacher and they were the students but Jesus, understanding his role as a disciple maker, had to move them forward and introduce them to life in the deep—a life surrendered to God that depends on him to lead the way. The crowd of hungry people in a remote place was an ideal opportunity to give them a glimpse of the truths found in a deeper and more intimate relationship with the Father. The men undoubtedly thought themselves proactive by bringing the situation to the attention of Jesus so he could resolve the problem. After all, throughout their travels he preached to the crowds, healed the sick, and performed miracles. Surely he would resolve this situation as well. But this time was different. Jesus turned up the spiritual thermostat and said, "You feed them." At that moment, the disciples had drifted into deeper water and found their feet coming off the bottom. Shock and panic welled up in their throats and out came their fear in words of confusion, self-doubt, and ignorance of how to fulfill his request. "That would take eight months of a man's wages! Are we to go and spend that much on bread and give it to them to eat?" In other words, "What? We can't possibly do that! We don't have enough money!" But Jesus does the very thing we as the church must do in order to help move people forward on their journey. He said, *"How many loaves do you have. Go and see."* Up to this point, the disciples had watched as Jesus worked miracles in front of them. It was time to pass the baton, but Jesus understood that they were not yet capable of making the miracle happen on their own. So he invited them to participate in the miracle with him. He created an opportunity for them to experience with him the kind of life that is possible beyond the fear barrier that existed in their minds.

Go and see opportunities allow people at stage four to brush shoulders with the ministry of their calling and take a "test drive" under the watchful eye of a discipler. This is possible when a church cultivates a culture that encourages and allows for ministry exploration. Every small group leader begins to see his or her group as a laboratory for those following the call of God. Every ministry leader begins to see his or her ministry as a go and see opportunity for those who are exploring their purpose and call. Servants are recruited with the understanding that saying yes does not mean they are locked in but instead are given permission to try it out.

The deep awaits each traveler like an unopened package waiting under the tree on Christmas morning. If the traveler never takes it, the package will go unopened. But, as we intentionally assist seasoned but restless believers in overcoming obstacles and fear of the unknown, they will be absolutely amazed by the gift that awaits them in stage five.

The primary components of stage four of the journey toward becoming a fully committed follower of Christ:

The primary person: Seasoned but restless believer
The primary question: Is there anything else?
The primary relationship: Small group leader and emerging discipler
The primary barriers: Fear, confusion, questioning his or her value, lack of direction
The primary ministry: Go and see

CHAPTER SIX

Stage Five: Life Beyond the Breakers

It was the second week in August 1987. I distinctly remember because it was the same week I turned thirty. My siblings and I were grown and each of us had families of our own. The three of us, along with our parents, gathered together for a family reunion at a rented ocean front house just south of the Outer Banks at Long Beach, North Carolina. I had vacationed at the ocean many times since my childhood days at Nags Head, but being there with my brother and sisters brought back a flood of fond memories. Now we were creating new memories with our own children.

We celebrated my birthday with too much cake and ice cream and lots of wonderful gifts. My brother-in-law, John, surprised me with the rental of a windsurfer. John, my brother Rick, another brother-in-law Doug and I excitedly planned a day of adventure in the ocean. The next morning, we hit the beach with gusto and complete confidence, despite the fact that none of us had any windsurfing experience. The board was rented for twenty-four hours, and we picked it up at 10:30 a.m. We took turns figuring out how to get on the board and sail a few feet before a wave would knock us off. By evening we were exhausted and decided to call it a day. The next morning we were up bright and early to get in a few more hours of fun before 10:30 rolled around and we had to return the board. We were in the water by 8:00, giving us a good two hours to play. By 9:30 each of us was actually pretty good at wind-surfing in shallow water. There was time for one more ride for each of us and the birthday boy was given the honor of riding last as our twenty-four hours rapidly came to a close.

My brother, Rick, stood in waist deep water and stabilized the board so I could jump on. I got my knees on the board and reached over to pull the sail and bring myself to a standing position. Just then I felt a little tug from an offshore breeze. I was still trying to raise the sail to full position when the board began to skim across the water without my realizing it. I turned to tell Rick he could let go and to my surprise he was fifty yards behind me. That little breeze had taken me straight away from the shore and toward the deep water of the Atlantic. My first thought was, "Cool! This will be a great last ride!" My second thought, accompanied by a twinge of fear, was, "Wow! This is moving faster than I expected," but I decided to keep going anyway. I knew I wasn't as experienced as I should be, but I accepted the risks that came with the ride.

It's amazing how far a windsurfer can travel in one minute with a sail full of wind! I could still see the beach and my three companions, but they were rapidly getting smaller. I attempted to turn the windsurfer around and finally dropped the sail by accident when I lost my balance in a large ocean swell. I went one way and the board went the other, and I found myself with ten feet between us. As I swam toward the board, I realized the sail was drifting in the opposite direction. Apparently I had knocked the pole loose when I fell off. "Funny how that never happened all those times we fell off the board in shallow water yesterday!" I thought to myself. I quickly chased down the sail and brought it back to the board. I noticed that water in the deep is much colder and more uncomfortable than water in the shallows.

I figured out how to reconnect the pole to the board and thought, "Good! I'm back in business." I aimed the board toward shore and hopped on. As I picked up the sail, the wind caught it, turned me like a compass needle looking for true north and began whisking me straight away from land toward the horizon. I tried everything I could think of to head back to the beach, but all I could see was the wake from the board as it sped away from shore. I fell off the board four or five more times in my futile attempts to turn around. Each time I fell off, the pole fell off the board as well. I found myself in the water one more time with the sail and pole drifting away when it again occurred to me just how cold the water really was that far off shore. I looked around and land was nowhere in sight. The enormity of the ocean began to overwhelm me. I was at the bottom of a huge swell with walls of water all around me. The fishing piers were far behind me and I had even passed beyond the path of the shrimp boats that troll the coastline. This was not the time to lose focus, so I set my sights on the sail and pole and swam toward them with great determination. When the next wave took me to the top of the swell, I caught a quick look at the shore. I was so far out that I couldn't identify individuals who were standing on the beach. They were just a bunch of little dots. My legs and arms were growing weaker by the minute and getting the sail to the board was much more difficult than before. As I reached out for the board, it almost playfully bobbed and scooted nearly fifteen feet away from me. I remember thinking that fifteen feet on dry land isn't much, but out here in deep water fifteen feet seemed like miles. Thoughts of how deep the water was below me began to take over. I pushed back the sickening feeling in my stomach and a surge of adrenaline moved me through the water to the board. I climbed on and began to remember that Jesus lingers just off the coastline of North Carolina. I know that's true because I met him there that day and we had a little chat right there on the windsurfer.

As I rose to the top of each swell, I looked toward the shore and it appeared that no one was doing much of anything about my predicament. They all apparently believed so much in my abilities as a former athlete that they were waiting for me to turn around and come back. But going back on my own was not an option. I had exhausted my knowledge of how to return, and the wheels of rescue needed to be set in motion. I was extremely tired, I was freezing, and I had no idea what might be lurking in the water below me. Fear was creeping toward me and I knew I had to maintain my focus. I decided to wave my hand in a way that would adequately convey the reality of my situation. "Frantically" would be a good way to describe it! John immediately dove into the surf. He was physically spent by the time he reached me, and now there were two of us clinging to the board far from shore. Nevertheless, his mere presence was a great source of comfort and we waited together for help to arrive.

Thank God for my years of experience at the ocean! During my time in the shallow water of the Outer Banks under the watchful eyes of my parents, I had learned about the awesome power of the ocean. I had learned to know when I was in control and when the ocean was in control. This was one of those times when the ocean was in control, and I had to choose to stop fighting against it and take a more appropriate course of action. I also thank God for my years of learning to know that Jesus is my refuge and my strength. He is the one on whom

I must focus my gaze or I run the risk of losing sight of what it is he wants me to accomplish. In this instance, that meant staying with the windsurfer so I didn't drown, even when cold and exhaustion began to take their toll. Like Peter stepping out of the boat, keeping my eyes on Jesus was the only thing that kept me from giving in to the panic and fear that tried to take me under. As frightening as the experience was at the time, I was able to move through the fear and come out on the other side with a greater knowledge of the deep and how to navigate there.

A lifeguard arrived shortly before the Coast Guard got there. The lifeguard and I paddled back to shore on his surfboard, John climbed aboard the rescue boat, and a female member of the Coast Guard jumped onto my windsurfer. She effortlessly rode it straight back to shore, speeding past the lifeguard and me and leaving us in her wake. I believe my male ego suffered the most damage from the experience. The Coast Guard told John I had drifted 1.25 miles from shore, was in water fifty-five feet deep, and had been out there for an hour and a half. Did I mention that water in the deep is much colder than water in the shallows?

The New Paradigm Follower

Stage five is represented by the person power stroking into deeper water. This is the person who has faced his or her fears and made the decision to move through them. The person at this stage is a new paradigm follower. No longer one who merely believes the promises of God, he or she is now one who has chosen to confront fear and trust that the promises are true. The vision of what God has in store is so compelling to the stage five person that he or she chooses to move ahead in spite of everything that could potentially cause emotional discomfort. Until that moment of decision is encountered, a person is only a believer. James 2:17 says, *"In the same way, faith by itself, if not accompanied by action, is dead."* There is an invisible but very real fear barrier that separates a person who is spiritually dog paddling and one who has chosen to move through the barrier into deeper water. On the shore side of the barrier, the obstacles seem insurmountable. There are not enough resources to make it feasible to go into the deep, and the vision seems impossible to accomplish. Complaining or trying to make it work some other way are still options to the dog paddler. However, once a person makes a conscious commitment to move forward and takes faith-based action steps, things happen that were not able to be seen on the fear-filled side of the barrier.

There is a John Maxwell quote taped inside my appointment book that speaks about this moment of decision to move beyond fear:

> "Until I am committed, there is a hesitancy, a chance to draw back. But the moment I definitely commit myself, then God moves also, and a whole stream of events erupt. All manner of unforeseen incidents, meetings, persons, material assistance that I could never have dreamed would come my way, begin to flow toward me—the moment I make a commitment."[1]

This is the abundance that exists in the inner life of a follower of Christ. This eruption of events awaits the person who opts to move beyond being a mere believer in God to becoming a spiritual commando who fearlessly pursues God's best.

The person at stage five experiences a paradigm shift. He or she no longer views life through the lens of unconquered fear but, instead, confronts the very things that paralyzed in the past, with hope-filled abandon. This new paradigm follower is what Paul was talking about when he wrote in First Thessalonians 1:7-8a, *"And so you became a model to all the believers in Macedonia and Achaia. The Lord's message rang out from you not only in Macedonia and Achaia—your faith in God has become known everywhere."* The person who breaks through the barrier

[1] *Leadership Wired,* March 2001.

into the open ocean begins to view life from a new perspective. Keeping one's own feet on the bottom is no longer the answer to keeping one's head above water. Now there is an expectation and reliance on God as the answer. When a stage five follower looks back toward the shoreline with all it's predictability and comfort, then looks toward unknown waters and knowingly choose to go there, the person is surrendering his or her life to the mercy of the deep and all that comes with it. If the person continues to surrender his or her will to God's greater plan, what life becomes from this point on is not his or her choosing but God's. Jesus says in Matthew 10:39, *"Whoever finds his life will lose it, and whoever loses his life for my sake will find it."* The stage five follower has made a choice to lose his or her life for the sake of Christ.

Where Has This Been All My Life?

At this stage, the primary question on the mind of the new paradigm follower who is released from the chains of fear and indecision is: "Where has this been all my life?" There is a lyric from the song *Already Gone* by The Eagles that says, "So often times it happens we live our lives in chains and never even know we have the key." The key to the abundant life is our willingness to choose to depend on God instead of depending on ourselves. It's putting our money where our mouth is as Christians. It's scary, but as unknown as this new territory is, the stage five follower knows it is where he or she is meant to be.

It's important to offer a warning. Simply following six easy steps will not magically transform a person into a fully committed follower with a deep and abiding relationship with the Creator. It is not possible to scan this process looking for a recognizable place in the progression, jump in where we think we might fit, and grab a tidbit or two that will help us "go deeper." To do so can put an unequipped person in danger of drowning. We cannot, in our own strength, jump ahead and rush into the deep. We must fully engage in the ministries, experience the relationships, wrestle with the hard questions, and overcome the barriers at each previous stage in order to live and thrive in the deep water of God's reality.

The church is asking for trouble when we allow new or rededicated believers to bypass the equipping that's needed to *effectively* follow God's call. Unfortunately, we not only allow it, we often encourage it. We find a willing servant with an interest or even a passion for a particular ministry and we put him or her in leadership without ever considering the extent to which the person is spiritually equipped. When that person struggles, we stand on the shore watching and waiting for him or her to get the chaos under control, just as my companions did while I repeatedly failed to control the windsurfer. We might complain about the lousy job the person is doing and, despite the fact that he or she needs direction and guidance from someone who has been in the same situation, we'll never say a word because that would be too confrontational. God knows "good Christians" aren't confrontational! Eventually, he or she self-destructs and becomes disillusioned with the local congregation and possibly the church in general. The clergy and senior lay leaders are either left surprised by what just happened, or they blame the failure on the unequipped ministry leader's character flaws.

The moment of moving through the fear barrier came for Peter in Acts 2:14. The Spirit of God had just descended on the disciples and they began speaking in the native tongues of all who had assembled in Jerusalem. As astounding as that might have first appeared to the crowd, they soon began to make fun of the disciples' strange and unfamiliar behavior. Just weeks before, Peter was faced with a choice, and he chose to deny that he even knew Jesus. That choice was based on fear—the primary barrier at stage four. Here he is once again facing an accusing crowd, but this time he makes an entirely different choice. It says in Acts 2:14, *"Then Peter stood up with the eleven, raised his voice and addressed the crowd."* I cannot over emphasize the mega-importance of that moment, not only in Peter's life, but also in the life of the church. He could have remained silent and been a footnote in the history books. Instead, he took what he knew to be the truth and proclaimed it to the same hostile crowd that only weeks earlier had crucified the one Peter now proclaimed as "Lord and Christ" (Acts 2:36). In this moment when choice moves to action, the stage four question, "Is there anything else?" melts away and the new paradigm follower sees a glimpse of God's bigger picture for his life. The power that accompanies that choice to move forward streams through his veins and he steps up to this new opportunity with renewed energy and desire.

The Discipler and the Holy Spirit

By standing up and addressing the mocking crowd, Peter moved firmly into stage five living, where one relies heavily on the primary relationships that help a person at this stage continue to move forward in his or her faith—the discipler and the Holy Spirit. The Holy Spirit has actually been involved in the spiritual development process all along but, until now, the traveler has not recognized him as a primary sustaining relationship. He or she has depended on a discipler for support. In this stage, however, he or she begins to understand that they work hand in hand. Look at how these two relationships sustained Peter. Jesus said in Luke 22:31, *"Simon, Simon. Satan has asked to sift you as wheat. But I have prayed for you, Simon, that your faith may not fail and, when you have turned back, strengthen your brothers."* This is specific direction and guidance Peter received from his discipler, Jesus. When combined with the electrifying confidence that came from being filled with the Holy Spirit, Peter was ready to "stand up and raise his voice" as the account records in the second chapter of Acts. The efforts of his discipler combined with the strengthening of the Holy Spirit formed a one-two combination that launched Peter through the fear barrier and into the deep.

There are many who have gone before us and stepped through the fear barrier. Look at Abraham at the altar with Isaac; Moses standing before Pharaoh; Joshua at the battle of Jericho; Gideon against the Midianites; Esther trusting that she was made for such a time as this; David fighting Goliath. But there are those who were less heroic but no less brave. There is Joseph who took the young pregnant Mary as his wife; the poor widow who gave her last two mites; Mary who broke the alabaster jar of nard over Jesus' feet. These are people, just like us, who have looked long and hard at the price they may have to pay for trusting God to sustain them and made the commitment to move forward anyway.

Lack of Focus and Discipline—Misinterpretation of Suffering

Once the fear barrier is penetrated, there are two obstacles faced by the person at stage five: a lack of focus and discipline, and the misinterpretation of suffering. In First Peter 4:17, Peter warns, *"Be self-controlled and alert. The devil prowls around like a roaring lion looking for someone to devour."* Writing from years of experience living beyond his fears, he is able to reflect and provides direction and guidance that a stage five person should heed. He warns to "be self-controlled (disciplined) and alert (focused)." The fear that threatened to overwhelm me the day the wind whisked me into the deep water off the coast of North

Carolina came from the sheer enormity of the ocean and my inability to know what lingered in the waters below. It was through the focus and discipline I had learned earlier in life that I was able to overcome the fear welling up in me, remain calm, and trust the outcome of my predicament to the Lord. The deep water of the Christian life can also be enormous and overwhelming, always moving toward an unknown future.

Matthew 14:27-31 teaches a lesson about both focus and discipline. Jesus came walking on top of the water toward the boat that carried the disciples across the Sea of Galilee. This passage records that they were all terrified when they saw him. This was a highly unnatural act, and I can't say that I blame them for being afraid.

> "Jesus immediately said to them, 'Take courage! It is I. Don't be afraid.' 'Lord, if it is you,' Peter replied, 'tell me to come to you on the water.' 'Come,' he replied. Then Peter got out of the boat, walked on the water and came toward Jesus. But when he saw the wind he was afraid and, beginning to sink, cried out, 'Lord, save me.' Immediately Jesus reached out his hand and caught him."

What Peter undoubtedly remembered from that experience was how it felt to move through his own fear and step away from the boat onto the surface of deep water with his gaze locked on Jesus all the way. As soon as Peter stopped focusing on Jesus and began paying attention to everything else (he "saw the wind") he began to sink. The lesson in this story is that we must discipline ourselves to keep our undivided focus on Christ if we are to sustain a long-term walk in the deep. The minute we pay attention to anything else, we go under.

The lack of focus and discipline is a constant source of trouble in the church. Typically, it happens like this: A new or rededicated believer begins attending church on a fairly regular basis. People approach him about helping out in some area of ministry. They are well intended in their invitation, believing that getting him involved is the way to make new friends and get connected to the life of the church. The new or rededicated believer is encouraged when his or her initial efforts are appreciated. He feels valued and wades deeper into the water by increasing his involvement. As he becomes more involved in various ministries and activities, he is exposed to more and more of the personal thoughts, feelings, and attitudes of the people he encounters. The thrill of being part of a community begins to wear off as he observes inconsistencies in the lives of the people he once thought were his greatest Christian role models. His focus on Christ and Christ alone as his example has not had the time to become the foundation of his faith. Nor has he had the opportunity to develop the discipline of daily seeking the guidance of the Holy Spirit and taking every thought captive for the sake of Christ. Soon, he finds himself quietly comparing the inconsistencies he sees in others with what he believes to be acceptable "good Christian" behavior. As this process continues, it gains momentum. Some become disenchanted and leave. Some become long term, silent critics who believe keeping their thoughts to themselves is the right thing to do. All the while, the resentment that builds up inside fries their spiritual lives to a crisp. Others opt for open verbal accusations as they strive to defend the church and expose all perceived inconsistencies and wrong doings to anyone with ears to listen. They actively poison the hearts and minds of all who listen to their righteous gossip and create general suspicion toward anything that does not conform to their image of what Christianity and the church "ought" to be. Undiscipled, unequipped believers breed unhealth in the church.

The ability to remain focused and disciplined is developed in the earlier stages of spiritual growth. In *The Lost Art of Disciple Making* (Zondervan: Grand Rapids, MI, 1978), author Leroy Eims seeks to answer the question, "How long does it take for a convert to become a disciple? A disciple a worker? A worker a leader?" He responds by saying, "Because people are so different from one another, the time elements will vary. But general guidelines can be suggested. They are convert to disciple - 2 years; disciple to worker - 2 years; worker to leader - 3 years." Note that Eims is suggesting that it takes *seven years* of intentional discipling to transform a new believer into an effective Christian leader. Do you see how we can stunt the spiritual growth of a person who becomes part of our congregation by involving him or her too early in significant positions of service? To insure a person's ability to maintain focus and discipline when he or she becomes deeply immersed in the body of Christ, we must emphasize spiritual development over service and activity and develop opportunities for learning and relational connection that are an irresistible attraction to new and rededicated believers. This will allow people time for Christ to be formed in them, knowing that God's call to service will beckon them in due time.

The second barrier in stage five is the misinterpretation of suffering. I venture to guess that this is the single biggest cause of spiritual fatalities in the church. It is very common, and typically goes unaddressed.

Here's the familiar scenario: You push past your fears and step out in faith, trusting God to sustain you. You give yourself wholly to the mission of Christ, you get out there and begin doing the work God has called you to do, then you take a fatal hit. It doesn't matter whether it's the first hit or the eighty-first hit. The one that will take you out is the one you take personally. The moment you take personally the attacks that are specifically intended to stop the mission of God from moving forward, you become a wounded body that will wash back toward the shore and become an easy target for any deep-dwelling shark to have for lunch. To correctly interpret the suffering that comes at this stage, one must understand that the mission of God produces conviction in the hearts of those who come in contact with it. This conviction is designed by God to move people out of their comfort zones, and that's extremely uncomfortable. And God knows emotional comfort is the number one goal for many! They typically can't describe what they are feeling when the spiritual agitation grinds inside them. All they know is where the discomfort is coming from, and their focus is fixed on you and the thing you are doing that is making waves. Maybe you change the children's curriculum, cleaned the sacred junk out of the attic without asking permission from the women's mission society, or launched a worship service with music that is more relevant to unchurched people. It doesn't matter. If you are not equipped in advance to correctly interpret the backlash by those who are fighting the conviction of the Holy Spirit, your ministry will be very short-lived. You will take it personally, and you will self-destruct.

Many called but unequipped followers wash back up on shore never to be heard from again. Some creep back into the church to begin again. In doing so, they again face the barriers at each stage of development starting with cynicism, moving into heightened sensitivity, and so on. Scripture says this offended sister is harder to win back than a fortified city. She's not going to be an easy sale, but this time she will be more cautious. If she is wise in her caution, she will learn more this time than she did before. If the church she chooses for her next attempt at the Christian life is prepared to equip her, she can go on to make a significant impact for the kingdom. If not, she will simply get involved in service and activity again and the pattern is likely to repeat itself.

It is critical that the stage five follower understands God's perspective on suffering. Let's look again at Jesus words to Peter in Luke 22:31:

"Simon, Simon. Satan has asked to sift you as wheat. But I have prayed for you, Simon, that your faith may not fail. And when you have turned back, strengthen your brothers." Jesus is forewarning Peter about the personal suffering that he is going to experience. In other words, Jesus is saying, "Look, Pete. Satan has his eye on you and he wants to take you apart. But I've been praying for you so you won't lose your faith while he's making your life miserable. Hang in there and after you've made it to the other side of the experience, make sure you tell others how to hang in there." It would be so much more comfortable if Jesus said something like, "I'm not gonna let him lay a hand on you!" but he didn't. He says suffering is part of God's plan, and he expects us to persevere. He doesn't sugar coat it or pull his punch. He makes it clear that living in the fullness of our God-given lives involves a sifting process. The suffering we encounter will act as a sieve to filter out any impurities in our lives. That's not what Satan wants, of course. He wants the suffering to break us and harden our hearts against any God-ordained action in our lives. When we misinterpret the suffering, take it personally and give up, Satan racks up another one for himself. When we correctly understand God's sifting process, the kingdom advances and the stage five follower experiences more and more of the abundant life even in the midst of trial.

Churches are notorious for misinterpreting the suffering of those who are attempting to follow their call. Too often, we rely on generalized, often counterfeit encouragement. "Gosh, that's too bad. I'll pray for you," we say as we go about our business and never give it another thought. But it sounded good! Or we simply remain silent and nod our heads in sympathetic resignation. In reality, what stage five people need is honest, direct feedback. The disciples learned from Jesus how to speak the truth in love that brings with it genuine encouragement and much needed direction and guidance. This is the heart of disciple making. Did the unequipped ministry leader I mentioned earlier self-destruct because of a character flaw? Could be. But the job of the church is not to toss that person aside and look for someone less flawed. Our job is to make disciples who learn to overcome their flaws.

Go and Make

When the stage five person moves through his or her fears, he or she is filled with renewed energy and desire and is ready to take action. The primary ministry for the person at this stage is opportunities to go and make. Jesus had poured himself and his teachings into the disciples. He had equipped them for his departure and then he clearly defined the mission. *"Therefore, go into all the world and make disciples of all nations . . . "* The disciples had been through Jesus' school of intentional discipleship and it was now time to put into practice all they had learned. They were commissioned to serve, to remember and put into use all he had taught them, and to surrender daily to the direction and guidance of the Holy Spirit. As a result, they would make disciples.

To effectively "go", a person must face his or her own fears and shortcomings and choose to move forward in spite of them. It means making "a searching and fearless personal, moral inventory", to use the terminology of Alcoholics Anonymous, and strive to overcome self-defeating behaviors. In doing so, he or she gains a more accurate self understanding, develops a healthier perspective of the fears that once paralyzed him or her, and enables the person to move ahead through the fear barrier. Gaining an accurate view of self defuses fear that can separate us from God and the future God has planned for us.

To effectively "make" requires a spiritual maturity that comes from an accurate view of God. Hebrews 5:14 says, *"But solid food is for the mature who, by constant use, have trained themselves to distinguish good from evil."* The solid food referred to in Hebrews is not simply deeper Bible study. The acquisition of intellectual knowledge alone will not develop us into mature followers. The solid food reserved for the mature follower is the knowledge we have put into "constant use" in deeper relationships. Our pews are filled with people who have acquired volumes of biblical knowledge. They may be able to quote chapter and verse and site historical facts from the works of Josephus, but they never apply it to themselves and put it to "constant use" in their day-to-day lives. Storing knowledge in our cranial memory banks means nothing. If, on the other hand, we take everything we learn about God from every source—sermons, classes, small groups, print and electronic media—and apply it every day along our journey, we will have a more accurate understanding of God when we arrive at stage five. Then we will be equipped to offer godly direction and guidance to those waiting to be discipled.

The position of Children's Ministry Coordinator was vacant, the kick off of new fall classes was just two weeks away, and the senior leadership of the church was in dire need of someone to take the helm. Joy was a layperson who believed God was calling her to that position.

She had served as a helper in children's ministry for several years, had management and training experience from the marketplace, was highly creative, and had a clear vision for the ministry. Joy was also a lifelong Christian who had spent years in classes and groups that had helped equip her for the deeper water of ministry leadership. She was hired on a trial basis at only a few thousand dollars a year to start with the promise that the salary would increase if both parties were satisfied with her performance. The job was enormous, and the pay was significantly less than a comparable job in the marketplace, but God had called her to it and she accepted.

Joy burst into tears her first week at work because she was afraid the job was too big for her. Her supervisor assured her that she would not be left on her own and they would make the journey together. Knowing from past experience that she could trust God to sustain her, she moved forward in spite of her fears **(1)**. She completely revamped the Sunday morning program from a traditional Sunday school format to a media-enhanced, high energy, large group experience with lots of singing, dancing, games, and activities that broke out into small groups of like-aged children with an adult shepherd to guide them. The children loved it, and they began inviting their friends. The church had what it always wanted: lots of children. But several people who had been part of the church for many, many years objected and complained. It was loud. It was noisy. The new format used too much space. The children were too rambunctious. Senior leadership helped deflect the complaints so Joy could continue to focus on ministry **(2)**. They interpreted the attacks so she would not take them personally **(3)**. The ministry continued to grow.

Eventually, it became apparent that Joy struggled with some self-defeating behaviors that threatened the success of the ministry. Many of Joy's key servants complained that she micro-managed and undermined their authority. Often, Joy would find herself at odds with her own servant workers and her personal "baggage" began to jeopardize the future of the ministry. Joy's supervisor lovingly confronted her about the issue and established an expectation that she overcome the problem in order to continue in the position **(4)**. Joy stepped up to the challenge and not only made a searching and fearless moral inventory but also took the necessary action steps to overcome her self-defeating behaviors **(5)**. She has grown into a top quality ministry leader and a more emotionally healthy Christian **(6)** as a result of being in a church that understands how to disciple a person at stage five. Let's break down her story and look at what transpired:

1. Joy stepped through the fear barrier.

2. She did not lose her focus on the mission of Christ, and church leadership partnered with her to deflect the objections of those who were uncomfortable with the forward movement of the mission.

3. She did not take the attacks personally, and church leadership helped interpret the verbal accusations for what they really were.

4. Church leadership did not stand by in silence when Joy got in over her head but, instead, lovingly confronted her, gave specific direction and guidance and held her accountable for the outcome.

5. Joy gained an accurate view of herself by facing her fears and shortcomings and choosing to move forward in spite of them by overcoming her self-defeating behavior.

6. She continues to gain an accurate view of God by putting into constant use everything she learned.

There is no other organization on earth but the church given the charge of carving out a pathway that equips men and women for the pursuit of God's call on their lives. If we don't do it, no one will.

The traveler who finds the courage to pass through the fear barrier begins the journey of a lifetime. As the traveler takes initial steps to live out God's calling, trusts in the Holy Spirit to sustain him or her, and navigates the dangerous water of the deep, his or her understanding begins to change. The traveler sees life from a Christian worldview instead of a cultural worldview and priorities shift. He or she begins to taste the abundant life and realizes that it is an inner life experienced in the invisible world of the spirit. But it's not the end of the road. Stage six lies ahead with the potential for ministry that can impact the world with larger than life results.

The primary components of stage five of the journey toward becoming a fully committed follower of Christ:

The primary person: New paradigm follower.

The primary question: Where has this been all my life?

The primary relationship: Discipler and the Holy Spirit

The primary barrier: Lack of focus and discipline and the misinterpretation of suffering.

The primary ministry: Go and make.

CHAPTER SEVEN

Stage Six: Life in the Deep

I learned about nitrogen narcosis while living in Florida. During a sermon illustration, the pastor at the church I attended asked the congregation if anyone knew the number one rule of SCUBA diving. Almost everyone responded, and I remember thinking so many must have known the correct answer because we lived in Florida. However, I've asked the same question throughout the country for the past fifteen years and discovered it makes no difference what state I'm in. People everywhere know the answer: Never dive alone. When using the buddy system, pairs of SCUBA divers dive together as a safety procedure that improves the divers' chances of avoiding or surviving accidents in or underwater. With buddy diving, each of the divers is presumed to have a responsibility to the other. The buddies are expected to monitor each other and stay close enough together to be able to help in an emergency. One of the dangers a buddy can help a diver avoid is nitrogen narcosis, or what Jacques Cousteau referred to as "rapture of the deep."

Here is what the online encyclopedia Wikipedia says about nitrogen narcosis:

> Nitrogen narcosis is a reversible alteration in consciousness that produces a state similar to alcohol intoxication in SCUBA divers at depths below 100 feet. At depths of 300 feet, it leads to hallucinations and unconsciousness. Its precise mechanism is not well understood, but it appears to be a direct effect of high nitrogen pressure on nerve transmission. The onset is hard to recognize, its severity is unpredictable, and it can kill from its own toxic effect or due to the resulting illogical behavior.

The most dangerous aspects of narcosis are the loss of decision-making ability, impaired judgment, and decreased coordination. The diver may start to feel invulnerable, disregarding normal safe diving practices. Frequently, divers throw away their masks and accelerate their descent to excessive depths. Affected divers may panic, sometimes remaining on the bottom, too exhausted to ascend. The syndrome may also cause exhilaration, giddiness, extreme anxiety, depression, or paranoia.

Although some divers seem to be able to cope with the symptoms and even claim to be less susceptible than others, tests have shown that all divers are affected by nitrogen narcosis.

I've had people tell me stories of their personal diving experiences that verify the reality of nitrogen narcosis. One watched his buddy take off his flippers and begin to walk on the ocean floor. When they finally got him to the surface, he said, "I knew I was almost out of air and had to go up, but I thought I had to walk out of the ocean." Another watched a diver strip off his tanks and descend to his death before anyone could reach him. These are tragic stories of those who were not mindful of the dangers of the deep.

There's something about the deep that woos us. It's as though we are hard wired to respond to the undeniable and alluring draw of the unknown. The writer of Ecclesiastes alludes to this in chapter 2, verse 10: *"God has placed eternity in the hearts of men."* This is the writer's way of describing that magnetic pull of the shepherd's voice that calls out to us to come further. God calls us to meet God in the deep places of the spirit and, for the person at this stage, there is no other choice but to go.

A Fully Committed Follower

The person at stage six is a fully committed follower. She didn't get there by accident but by choice. She chose to surrender everything to the journey God unfolds before her. She spent adequate time in the shallows and chose to learn the truth about herself and God. She chose to develop intimate, trusting relationships and to allow those relationships to work as God's tools in the remolding of her life. She chose to face fears she never thought she could overcome. And she chose to allow God to transform her until she could see the world from a new perspective. At this stage, she *must* follow God's call because she cannot *not* follow it! Women and men who dwell in the deep and abiding presence of their creator make a significant difference in the lives of those they touch because they choose to make Jesus and the mission of God the central focus of their lives. Everything is affected by the centrality they place on Christ. No longer is Jesus an afterthought or even an extra thought. Jesus *is* the thought!

A fully committed follower has surrendered both his personal life and his call to Christ. He has made the choice to allow God's transforming power to mold him more and more into the likeness of Christ no matter what. Whatever suffering he may endure in the process is worth the discomfort and sacrifice. He can say along with Paul in Galatians 2:20, *"I have been crucified with Christ and I no longer live, but Christ lives in me. The life I live in the body, I live by faith in the son of God who loved me and gave himself for me."* The stage six person has died to his own agenda and, instead, makes himself available for whatever purpose God has planned. Mother Theresa said, "I belong to Jesus. He must have the right to use me without consulting me."

Fully committed followers carry with them a message that is irresistible. People are drawn to it often for reasons they can't explain. This attractiveness is often misidentified as a charismatic personality, but it goes beyond that. At this stage of spiritual development, the message and the messenger are so inseparable it is difficult to tell the difference. However, the fully committed follower understands and remembers it is not him or her who is attractive but the truth of God that has taken up permanent residence within.

What Do You Want Me To Do, Lord?

The primary question on the mind of a fully committed follower is, "What do you want me to do, Lord?" It sounds very much like the question, "How can I help?" that was asked back in stage three, doesn't it? The difference, however, is in the motivation. "How can I help?" springs from a personal need to connect and contribute. "What do you want me to do, Lord?" springs from a choice to surrender to God and a desire to obey God. The stage six person has come to the conclusion that God and God's mission are the primary focus of life and has chosen to be in absolute pursuit of both. A fully committed follower of Christ never stops. He or she only reloads.

When God replies to our question, "What do you want me to do, Lord?" God's expectation is that we will be obedient. If we've learned our lessons along the way, we will practice the focus and discipline that is required to stay on course and guard against spiritual attack. In First Corinthians 9:26-27, Paul describes it this way, *"Therefore I do not run like a man running aimlessly; I do not fight like a man beating the air. No, I beat my body and make it my slave so that after I have preached to others, I myself will not be disqualified for the prize."* He is telling us that the need for focus and discipline is greater, not less, for those who progress to stage six, and the possibility of disqualification from completing the mission is very real. As is true at every stage, there is an increased risk of self-destruction if we are not mindful of the barriers. We have all witnessed spiritual leaders who, for one reason or another, have found themselves in a position where they either drifted away or walked away from their God-assignment because they lost focus, took their eyes off the goal, and allowed distractions to divert their attention.

There will be many important things that have the potential to distract us along the way. Financial set backs, family members in crisis who need our attention, bureaucratic red tape, family or friends who are unsupportive or intentionally work against us, physical set backs, etc. Sometimes the distractions come in the form of alternative pursuits that seem to be just the thing that would please God but are not what God has called us to be about. I have to admit, I allowed myself to get caught up in the dream of a friend, and spent two years up to my elbows in the development and launch of a 501c3 non-profit outreach to unchurched students and young adults. Just the kind of stuff God loves, right? That might be true, but it was not what God has called me to do. I allowed that "good thing" to distract me from the development and nurture of the discipleship pathway at the church where I work. The non-profit had painfully struggled through two managers and never really got on its feet. When I finally realized that I was outside God's will for my life, I made the decision to refocus and shut down the ministry. Within one month of turning my attention back to the assignment God had given me, my energy for the mission increased and neglected areas of ministry began to resuscitate. As numerous, varied, and persistent as distractions may be, the primary barrier at this stage is even more formidable.

Isolation

Innocent but potentially dangerous thoughts develop in the minds of people who surround a person at stage six. They see a deep and abiding contentment that comes from Christ reflected in the fully committed follower, and he or she appears to lack for nothing. They think, "Now there's someone who really has his act together." They believe any input from them would not only be unnecessary but also unwelcome. They don't want to insult the stage six person so they don't speak up. Others watch from a distance and stay at arms length because they fear getting too close might reveal a sharp spiritual contrast they don't want to see between the person and themselves. You've heard the comments. "I could never pray aloud in front of her. She would think I sound stupid." "I wouldn't dream of bothering him. He has far more important things to do than talk to me." These beliefs on the part of others contribute to the primary barrier faced by the person at this stage—isolation.

But self-generated isolation lurks in the shadows as well. Real trouble begins when the fully committed follower entertains the same dangerous thoughts as those around him or her. If he is not mindful of the treacherous water in which he finds himself, the stage six person can begin to believe he is so complete in Christ that he doesn't need anything from anyone. She can begin to believe that she has arrived; she's grabbed the brass ring and there's nothing left to do but bask in the glory of the winner's circle. If the primary question—"What do you want me to do, Lord?"—is misinterpreted and used as justification for resisting the wise counsel of others, the fully committed follower can develop a formidable independence that renders him unaccountable and unteachable. "After all," he says to himself, "God is guiding me. What more do I need to know?"

We are all painfully aware of the tragic and very public self-destruction of Jimmy Swaggart and Jim Bakker. But you and I are also familiar with the men and women in our own communities who are currently self-destructing right before our eyes.

- A woman had been a member of the church family from the time there were several hundred in weekly worship, and she helped develop a vibrant ministry that grew the church to 2,500 in attendance. As a middle manager, she supervised a team of people who offered new, exciting, cutting edge suggestions for effective ministry. She received the suggestions politely, but continued to follow the same course she had taken in previous years. The church's senior leadership expected more out of her department but it never materialized. She was genuinely surprised when she was fired.

- A pastor led his congregation to a significant level of effectiveness and grew it to a point where he could no longer manage the expanding ministry himself. He hired new staff and delegated responsibilities. Unfortunately, he would not release control. He undermined the authority of the very ones he hired and micro managed them at every turn. He rejected the advice and counsel offered by others and insisted that he knew what he was doing. After all, he had led the church this far, hadn't he? Eventually, wounded and battle-weary leaders began leaving the church in search of another that would offer emotionally healthy leadership. The day came when he found most of his leaders gone.

- A small group coach joined the Small Group Director for a meeting with one of the small group leaders who was experiencing difficulties with his group and needed constructive direction and guidance. Before the Director could open his mouth, the coach blasted the small group leader with a barrage of reprimands for his poor leadership, and chastised him for not doing a better job of controlling his people. The small group leader left the meeting in an emotional heap. The stunned Director asked the coach how he thought the meeting went. The coach replied, "I think it went quite well." "Let's talk about your approach for a minute," said the Director but, before he could say another word, the coach interrupted. "Are you questioning my leadership?" he defiantly asked. He then proceeded to defend his actions, and also criticized the Director's leadership of the ministry. He was soon removed from his position as small group coach.

- A man who served on the leadership board of his former church left after fifty years of membership because the pastor refused to be held accountable. "I am accountable to God. I don't need to be accountable to men," the pastor stated to his board. The church became stagnant under his leadership, and angry, disillusioned parishioners left in search of a church with biblical leadership.

If the fully committed follower resists or does not seek biblical input from others, she runs the risk of improperly discerning God's voice in the clamor of full impact ministry. Disqualification comes when she chooses over the long haul to cling tightly to "my way" and falls out of God's will. Her ministry may creep along but, eventually, she is taken out or she takes herself out of any form of ministry that effectively offers life transformation.

The fully committed follower will experience close communion with God and some degree of success in living out his call. When the arena in which his call is lived out is public, or the ministry has broad impact, there is an appropriate level of protectiveness that should exist to guard the stage six person from exploitation by others. However, if he dives into the deep water of this stage alone and becomes isolated, all the symptoms of "spiritual nitrogen narcosis" begin to appear. Let's look at the symptoms again but, this time, filter them through your recollections of spiritual leaders (both lay and clergy) who have self-destructed:

> The onset is hard to recognize, its severity is unpredictable, and it can kill from its own toxic effect or due to the resulting illogical behavior.
> The most dangerous aspects . . . are the loss of decision-making ability, and impaired judgment . . . (He or she) may start to feel invulnerable, disregarding normal safe . . . practices. Frequently (unequipped stage six followers) throw away their masks and accelerate their descent to excessive depths. Affected (stage six followers) may panic, sometimes remaining on the bottom, too exhausted to ascend. The syndrome may also cause exhilaration, giddiness, extreme anxiety, depression, or paranoia.

Although some (stage six followers) seem to be able to cope with the symptoms and even claim to be less susceptible than others, tests have shown that **all . . . are affected by nitrogen narcosis.**

Did you catch that? All are affected. If you have identified yourself as a fully committed follower who is on the verge of crash and burn, don't panic because "nitrogen narcosis is a *reversible* alteration in consciousness." Just as in the case of SCUBA divers, stage six followers can avoid a painful crash and burn by intentionally equipping themselves through the use of the buddy system.

When using the buddy system, pairs . . . dive together as a safety procedure that improves (their) chances of avoiding or surviving accidents . . . (and) each . . . is presumed to have a responsibility to the other. The buddies are expected to monitor each other and stay close enough together to be able to help in an emergency.

Your buddy will be found in the primary relationships for a person at this stage. Those relationships are both internal and external. They are the Holy Spirit and the authentic spiritual community.

The Holy Spirit Brings Comfort

Believers in the earlier stages of their journey experience an earthly comfort derived from human relationships, their environment, and their circumstances. God draws them from that zone of comfort into risk-taking relationship with Jesus. At this stage, however, God makes provision for spiritual comfort for those who surrender to God. At stage six, comfort is no longer derived from the physical realm but from the guidance received from the Holy Spirit. In fact, as we see in the lives of the disciples and the apostle Paul, God redefines comfort. When a person at this stage is aligned with God's purpose and plan, there comes a stability that gives an entirely new meaning to comfort. Jesus spoke clearly to his disciples about the Holy Spirit and his purpose for coming. John 16:7b (American Standard Version) says, " . . . *for if I go not away, the Comforter will not come unto you; but if I go, I will send him unto you."* John 16:13a goes on to say, *"But when he, the Spirit of truth, comes, he will guide you into all truth."* Living in the truth of God's presence and purpose is where a fully committed follower finds comfort.

The Holy Spirit Brings Power

After three years of intense personal discipleship, Jesus was ready to entrust the future of Christianity to the disciples. He instructed them as to how they would be able to accomplish such a daunting task in Acts 1:8. *"And you will receive power when the Holy Spirit comes upon you and you will be my witnesses in Jerusalem, Judea, Samaria and to the uttermost parts of the earth."* John 16:13b says, *"He will not speak on his own; he will speak only what he hears, and he will tell you what is yet to come."* In other words, the disciples' relationship with the Holy Spirit was to be their source of direction, guidance, and power to accomplish the mission. A fully committed follower understands and embraces this relationship. While every stage six person will not have global impact in "Jerusalem, Judea, Samaria and to the uttermost parts of the earth", every fully committed follower will have significant impact in, at least, their own corner of the world. How far reaching their impact will be is up to God alone, and God's plan and purpose will be revealed through the Holy Spirit by leading the fully committed follower "into all truth."

The Authentic Spiritual Community

The authentic spiritual community is "Jesus with skin on" in the life of a fully committed follower, but it's not just a bunch of deep dwellers high fiving each other over their latest ministry accomplishments. Look closely at the biblical accounts and you will see this community emerge from the beginning to the end of the spiritual journey. The authentic spiritual community consists of people at each stage who are leaning forward in search of God's truth in the deep water of the Spirit. They are the ones who are hungry for more. Think about it. Who are the people you find most encouraging and uplifting? Who are the ones that make you say, "Oh, yea! Now I remember why I do this." Is it an unchurched person passionately seeking the truth, or a stage three believer who has settled into his comfort zone and become a rule-bound pew sitter? Is it the curious person at stage two who innocently but genuinely asks, "How can I help?", or a fully committed follower who keeps everyone at arms length and resists wise counsel?

Numerous examples of the authentic spiritual community pop out of scripture.

Uncurched: Matthew 15:21-28 describes an unchurched woman in searched of the truth. In spite of Jesus' initial resistance to her pleas, her hunger for the truth drove her to keep coming at him. Here persistence was irresistible to him.

"Leaving that place, Jesus withdrew to the region of Tyre and Sidon. A Canaanite woman from that vicinity came to him, crying out, 'Lord, Son of David, have mercy on me! My daughter is suffering terribly from demon possession.' Jesus did not answer a word. So his disciples came to him and urged him, 'Send her away for she keeps crying out after us.' He answered (to the woman), 'I was sent only to the lost sheep of Israel.' The woman came and knelt before him. 'Lord, help me!' she said. He replied, 'It is not right to take the children's bread and toss it to their dogs.' 'Yes, Lord,' she said, 'but even the dogs eat the crumbs that fall from their master's table.' Then Jesus answered, 'Woman, you have great faith! Your request is granted.' And her daughter was healed from that very hour."

Curious: Zacchaeus is the epitome of the curious person in search of the truth but hover at the fringes of the crowd.

"Jesus entered Jericho and was passing through. A man was there by the name of Zacchaeus; he was a chief tax collector and was wealthy. He wanted to see who Jesus was but, being a short man, he could not because of the crowd. So he ran ahead and climbed a sycamore-fig tree to see him since Jesus was coming that way. When Jesus reached the spot, he looked up and said to him, 'Zacchaeus, come down immediately. I must stay at our house today.' So he came down at once and welcomed him gladly. All the people saw this and began to mutter, 'He has gone to be the guest of a sinner.' But Zacchaeus stood up and said to the Lord, 'Look, Lord! Here and now I give half of my possessions to the poor and if I have cheated anybody out of anything, I will pay back four times the amount.' Jesus said to him, 'Today salvation has come to this house because this man, too, is a son of Abraham. For the Son of Man came to seek and to save what was lost'" (Luke 19:1-10).

New or Rededicated Believer: While stage three believer, Martha, chose to help, Mary chose to spend time with Jesus and learn. Jesus encouraged and supported her decision.

"As Jesus and his disciples were on their way, he came to a village where a woman named Martha opened her home to him. She had a sister called Mary who sat at the Lord's feet listening to what he said. But Martha was distracted by all the preparations that had to be made. She came to him and asked, 'Lord, don't you care that my sister has left me to do the work by myself? Tell her to help me!' 'Martha, Martha,' the Lord answered, 'you are worried and upset about many things, but only one thing is needed. Mary has chosen what is better and it will not be taken away from her'" (Luke 10:38-42).

Seasoned But Restless Believer: Nicodemus was obviously a seasoned believer who was driven by his spiritual agitation to go further in his understanding of Jesus. His fear of backlash from other "teachers of the law" resulted in a nocturnal visit. John 3:1-4 says,

"Now there was a man of the Pharisees named Nicodemus, a member of the Jewish ruling council. He came to Jesus at night and said, 'Rabbi, we know you are a teacher who has come from God. For no one could perform the miraculous signs you are doing if God were not with him.' In reply Jesus declared, 'I tell you the truth, no one can see the kingdom of God unless he is born again.' 'How can a man be born when he is old?' Nicodemus asked. 'Surely he cannot enter a second time into his mother's womb to be born!'"

Jesus went on to explain the truth to his sincere and willing listener.

New Paradigm Follower: As you read Mark 5:1-13 & 19-21, take note that the natural response of being delivered through the fear barrier is an overwhelming passion to get closer to Jesus and a declaration of, "Where has this been all my life?" to those who surround a new paradigm follower.

"They went across the lake to the region of the Gerasenes. When Jesus got out of the boat, a man with an evil spirit came from the tombs to meet him. This man lived in the tombs and no one could bind him anymore, not even with a chain. For he had often been chained hand and foot, but he tore the chains apart and broke the irons on his feet. No one was strong enough to subdue him. Night and day among the tombs and in the hills he would cry out and cut himself with stones. When he saw Jesus from a distance, he ran and fell on his knees in front of him. He shouted at the top of his voice, 'What do you want with me, Jesus, Son of the Most High God? Swear to God that you won't torture me!" (Sure sounds like a guy facing fear to me!) For Jesus said to him, 'Come out of this man, you evil spirit!

"Then Jesus asked, 'What is your name?' 'My name is Legion,' he replied, 'for we are many.' And he begged Jesus again and again not to send them out of the area.

"A large herd of pigs was feeding on the nearby hillside. The demons begged Jesus, 'Send us among the pigs; allow us to go into them.' He gave them permission and the evil spirits came out and went into the pigs. The herd, about two thousand in number, rushed down the steep bank into the lake and were drowned.

"As Jesus was getting into the boat, the man who had been demon-possessed begged to go with him. Jesus did not let him, but said, 'Go home to your family and tell them how much the Lord has done for you and how he has had mercy on you.' So the man went away and began to tell in the Decapolis (10 cities) how much Jesus had done for him. And all the people were amazed."

Fully Committed Follower: Fully committed followers reveal themselves through their surrender and unwavering faith.

"When Jesus entered Capernaum, a centurion came to him asking for help. 'Lord,' he said, 'my servant lies at home paralyzed and in terrible suffering.' Jesus said to him, 'I will go and heal him.' The centurion replied, 'Lord, I do not deserve to have you come under my roof. But just say the word and my servant will be healed. For I myself am a man under authority with soldiers under me. I tell this one 'Go,' and he goes; and that one 'Come,' and he comes. I say to my servant, 'Do this,' and he does it. When Jesus heard this, he was astonished and said to those following him, 'I tell you the truth, I have not found anyone in Israel with such great faith. I say to you that many will come from the east and the west and will take their places at the feast with Abraham, Isaac and Jacob in the kingdom of heaven. But the subjects of the kingdom will be thrown outside into the darkness where there will be weeping and gnashing of teeth.' Then Jesus said to the centurion, 'Go! It will be done just as you believed it would.' And his servant was healed at that very hour" (Matthew 8:5-13).

Following the Holy Spirit "into all truth" allows the fully committed follower to discern those who are part of the authentic spiritual community from those who are inauthentic and may exploit us if we misplace our trust in them. Jesus was clear about the difference between these two groups. He could sniff out the hidden agendas of the Pharisees and Sadducees and had no tolerance for either. Jesus said to the paralytic in Matthew 9, *"Take heart, son, your sins are forgiven."* He was living out God's plan and purpose for him—to remove sin as an obstacle between God and his people. But verse 3 says, *"At this, some teachers of the law said to themselves, 'This fellow is blaspheming!' Knowing their thoughts, Jesus said, 'Why do you entertain evil thoughts in your hearts?'"* Jesus immediately recognized the lack of authenticity among those who clung tightly to rules and regulations and ignored the power of authentic truth-seeking relationship that was right before their eyes. It was obvious they discounted Jesus because he did not fit into their preconceived religious box and, in doing so, identified themselves as people who had settled into their comfort zones and become rule-bound pew sitters. Jesus had no desire and felt no obligation to make friends with these teachers of the law. Being a "good Christian boy" who did not make waves had no place in his life. His pursuit of God's truth was his only goal, he kept himself from isolation by doing life with those who shared an authentic quest for that same truth, and he guarded himself from those who sought to exploit him. He judged the condition of their hearts before he made his decision, and so should every fully committed follower.

One-On-One Discipling

Those who make up the authentic spiritual community embrace a holy anticipation about the future when in the presence of a fully committed follower. They sense something coming and look forward to it with great anticipation. They have a desire to give themselves fully to the mission of God at whatever stage they find themselves because of that follower's influence. Together they know the future is secure, the present risks are high, reaching the goal will require total commitment, and life is abundant. This is discipleship at it's finest.

Somewhere in the authentic spiritual community is another fully committed follower who is God's provision for the stage six person. These are powerful relationships that make up the primary ministry to the person who is out in the deep, where few will venture except for other fully committed spiritual warriors. That primary ministry is one-on-one discipling, the spiritual buddy system that keeps a fully committed follower from self-destructing.

Scripture describes this one-on-one relationship:

> "The purposes of a man's heart are deep waters, but a man of understanding draws them out" (Proverbs 20:5).

The writer of Proverbs is defining the nature of the relationship. In the heart of every person is the unique purpose for which they were created. Before we were born, that purpose was placed in each of us and it waits to be discovered. It takes the experienced and skillful life of another to help draw it to the surface.

"A man of many companions may come to ruin, but there is a friend who sticks closer than a brother" (Proverbs 18:24).

This relationship demands deep trust, genuine acceptance as well as time and patience. It demands a willingness and ability to hold each other accountable, not to rules and regulations but to God's truth.

"A friend loves at all times, and a brother is born for adversity" (Proverbs 17:17).

This relationship is born out of pure intentions for the spiritual, emotional, and physical health of the receiver. The giver must not be impressed by the receiver or hold him or her in awe; the giver must not be intimidated by the receiver. The giver must be objective and forthright. When adversity comes, this relationship will stand as an anchor in the middle of the storm.

I am a premier advocate of small group discipleship, but there comes a time in the spiritual journey of many when small group life will take them no further. These verses help explain why a group of people simply cannot affect a stage six person the way one other fully committed risk-taking warrior can. We all need someone to show us the ropes when we attempt to go where we've never been before. We need someone with experience to point out the land mines and barriers, to help interpret the environment and the circumstances. We need a buddy to successfully navigate the deep. Within the circle of the twelve disciples, Jesus regularly pulled three, Peter, James and John, out of this small group for experiences that indicate he had a deeper relationship with them than with the others. The deeper relationship he had with John was one of such trust that he could confidently pass on the responsibility for his mother just prior to his death. His intimate relationship with Peter resulted in warning of Satan's impending sifting, and instruction to become a "stage six buddy" by returning and strengthening his brothers.

Jesus' death broke up the comfort of the disciples' small group because the disciples were ready to face the purpose for which they were put on this planet. When he stated on the cross, *"It is finished"* (John 19:30), he was referring not only to his life, but also to the work that had been accomplished through him in the lives of the disciples. They were trained to go and make disciples of all nations and would have to find those who would be their anchors. The deep is not crowded, but fully committed followers must choose their buddies wisely.

Obviously, one-on-one discipling at this stage is an intensely personal ministry between two people. Therefore, we as church leaders cannot package it and dictate who should be in a one-on-one relationship with whom. Do not misunderstand. We are not suggesting that a ministry in which more mature believers individually disciple those newer to their faith is inappropriate. It is, in fact, desirable. In this instance, however, we are speaking of fully committed followers only.

What the church can do for people at this stage is create a culture of one-on-one accountability through structures that include pastoral accountability to the leadership board or elders, and staff supervision of every ministry leader. In creating a culture that values one-on-one discipling[1], the church encourages and establishes an expectation that all spiritual travelers will avoid making the journey in isolation. With these structures in place, those who attempt to go it alone can be identified more quickly and redirected to a more healthy and positive course of action.

God is never finished with fully committed followers. God is constantly calling and challenging us to go further. Each time we choose to follow, we experience the ebb and flow of the tide and again encounter fear barriers to overcome and suffering to endure. We must constantly remain focused and disciplined. But, what a life! As we free fall into God's arms and submit to God's will, our lungs will be filled to capacity with the wind of the Spirit. Keep going. The journey is worth it.

A Note to Professional Clergy

You are men and women who have allowed the call of God to pull you away from shore. All of you have faced fears and asked your families to face those fears with you. Many of you have given up successful careers in the marketplace. If you had it to do over again, some of you might choose a different path. But here you are, fully engaged in professional ministry as a clergyperson.

Most pastors will describe themselves spiritually as somewhere in the deep. They will point to the times they moved through fear barriers and endured suffering. They will say they have laid it all on the line for Christ, and they will point to some victory of which they have been

---

[1]Discipleship consists of encouragement, the confession of dreams, fears and desires . . . not just sin, direction and guidance, accountability, and loving confrontation.

a part. But after declaring the virtues of their local congregation and sharing evidence of its vitality (usually worship attendance numbers that include everyone but the neighborhood cat, or membership numbers if they are larger), their words drift off and they glance away from my gaze.

I know what you're thinking because I've been where you are. I can hear your thoughts. "I want to be a risk-taking follower, but my life is so utterly predetermined by the demands of the ministry. God has given me a vision and I can see it. I might even be able to articulate it. I see the benefit and community-impacting potential of a church filled with discipled followers, but I'm drowning in day-to-day details as it is. I don't have time to pull off a mass movement of people from the pews into deep water. Besides, most of them won't like it and will resist. And when they do, they will verbally attack me. When that happens, I will have to suffer the consequences and that would be very hard on my family."

That may not be exactly what you are thinking but, for many of you, I'll bet I'm hitting pretty close to home. Here's the bad news. You are already suffering, but it's from nitrogen narcosis that has begun to distort your view of reality as you look out over your congregation. Most of your people are dying for you to lead them to a place they've never been before. Will there be resistance by a minority? Of course! There will always be those who never adopt new ideas and loudly resist change. So what? Christ didn't die so we could be safe and comfortable while our parishioners drift into numbness. He died to save the world and he issued us our marching orders. Go and make disciples. I can't begin to count the number of pastors who tell me that new ideas will work at someone else's church or in a new church plant, but not in their established congregation. It's a lie . . . and Satan is thrilled when we buy into it. It's not the truth.

The second part of this book offers you a tool. That tool is a discipleship pathway, a map that can be used by every church of any size in every denomination to put into place in the proper sequential order the ministries you've just read about at each of the six stages of spiritual development. The ministries in your church may not look exactly like the ministries in the church down the road, even if you both follow this pathway to the letter. This is a pathway that incorporates the "DNA" of your church. In other words, your pathway will look like you. You can build it in your time frame and move as quickly or as slowly as you like. And, as you incorporate the discipleship pathway into the day-to-day life of your congregation, you will slowly begin to see more and more of your people wade into deeper spiritual water.

When I assess the value and strategic impact of a course of action for the church, I ask myself, "Would Christ have died for this?" Very often the answer is no. He didn't die for every good thing we think we want to do. He died for the truth of the gospel. When we commit ourselves to anything other than that truth as revealed in scripture, we settle for ineffective ministry.

I believe the local congregation can be the answer to the decline of the church's influence on the culture. Jesus assures us in John 19:12, "*I tell you the truth, anyone who has faith in me will do what I have been doing. He will do even greater things than these because I am going to the Father.*" If we, the bride of Christ, choose to believe him and fearlessly look to our groom and allow him to show us how he made disciples, we can make a transformational difference. No matter the size of the congregation, we can fulfill our commission and effectively make disciples. The shepherd is calling us into the deep. Will you go?

The primary components of stage six of the journey toward becoming a fully committed follower of Christ:

The primary person: Fully committed follower.

The primary question: What do you want me to do, Lord?

The primary relationship: The Holy Spirit and the authentic spiritual community.

The primary barrier: Isolation.

The primary ministry: One-on-one discipling.

CHAPTER EIGHT

The Discipleship Pathway

I was once sort of lost in the woods. Please understand that I knew where I was and where I was going. I even thought I knew how to get there, but I didn't. So I wasn't actually lost as much as I was mistaken and confused. Here's what happened. My wife, Kathy, and I traveled to the overlook in Cooper's Rock State Park in West Virginia, along with two friends. I love hiking and spending time in the woods! It was a beautiful day, so I was hesitant to go straight back to the car when we had our fill of looking out over the view we had come to experience. I came up with the idea that we could hike back to the park entrance while our two friends drove back. It would mean they would have a short wait while we made our way there and, since they were not avid hikers, they readily agreed. As they headed for the car, we launched into the woods.

My plan was to cut cross-country and, because I am a visionary and not an implementer, I truly believed we would beat the car back to the entrance. As big-picture visionaries often do, I underestimated what it was going to take to get from here to there. The terrain turned out to be different than I imagined, and we carried no navigational equipment. In spite of those liabilities, I believed I knew exactly where I was going and I confidently announced that the highway leading to the park's entrance was just around every turn and over every hill. Unfortunately, the highway and therefore the entrance, never materialized. Two hours after parting ways with our friends, I had led my wife to the top of an impassable gorge, snow was beginning to fall, and darkness was closing in. I stared out over that gorge as reality sank in and realized I had depleted my supply of positive and uplifting "we're almost there" statements. The only thing we could do was retrace our steps and return the way we came if we ever hoped to get to the warmth and safety of the car. Five and a half hours after going our separate ways, we finally arrived and found our faithful friends worried sick but still waiting.

I understood the beauty of the woods that surrounded us and had knowledge of the environment. I knew where I was when I started and where I wanted to go. I also had hiking experience and understood the general direction I needed to take to reach my destination. However, it was not clear to me which turns to make and what hills to climb. I could only guess what to do next, and I really thought I could figure it out as I went along. It would have saved all of us a lot of time, energy, and wrong turns if only I had a map. Oh, I finally got to my destination, but I had to backtrack and repeat my steps in order to get there. When we finally arrived, we were exhausted, freezing, and in pain. It was not a positive experience.

We've heard similar stories from numerous pastors as they've told about their years of leading local congregations. All have had good, noble intentions when they started their careers. Each one began with an understanding of where he or she was and where he or she wanted to take the church. Each wanted to be part of building a great work for God. Every one of them had several great ideas and the encouragement of their friends and families, so they launched off into the woods, blazing a trail with all the fire of the early church pioneers. But months, years, decades later, they found themselves at an impasse. They had enjoyed some beautiful scenery and memorable experiences, but they were lost in the spiritual woods, walking in circles, following the church calendar and hoping each year would be the one when the entrance to the park would appear finally around the next bend.

We will often spot teary-eyed men and women speckled throughout the crowd as we present a seminar explaining the ocean diagram. The piercing truth of the scripture brings emotion right to the surface as people begin to see the progressive revelation of biblically based disciple making. Many have felt they finally found the underlying philosophy that will allow them to go back to their churches and develop a discipleship structure that can bring about real life transformation. A few have experienced limited success as they've implemented those pieces that made sense to them, but most have struggled to find the right combination of offerings and the right order in which to offer them. Taking philosophy and concept and turning it into a tangible product that can be effectively implemented requires a particular gift-mix and a significant outlay of time and energy. A map to follow can make the journey much more possible. With a map, we can know which hills to climb. More people can actually arrive at the desired destination. A map shows what's coming down the road so we can avoid wrong turns. The discipleship pathway is just such a map.

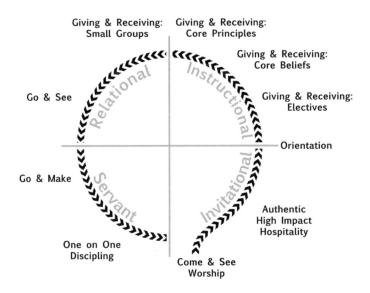

In this image, the circle represents the body of Christ. The arrowheads represent the pathway that moves through the life of the church and points the way toward deeper relationship with God. The steps along the pathway are ministries in the church that correspond to the six stages of spiritual development through which a person travels on the journey toward becoming a fully committed follower.

The discipleship pathway is broken into four sections, each one representing the "type" of discipleship that meets the changing needs of the traveler as he or she develops and matures in faith. There sections are:

• Invitational Discipleship;

• Instructional Discipleship;

- Relational Discipleship;

- Servant Discipleship.

Each of the four sections is made up of specific ministries that have a significant and positive impact on the traveler at his or her particular stage of development. The pathway flows counterclockwise from "come and see"—the point at which the path of an unchurched person intersects with the path of the church, to "one-on-one"—the buddy system that keeps a fully committed follower focused on God's purpose in his or her life. The objective of each ministry is to help overcome the barriers that keep people from moving forward.

In the first half of this book, we identified the "primaries" at each stage of spiritual development:

- The primary person traveling along the pathway.

- The primary question he or she is entertaining at each stage.

- The primary relationships the traveler needs within the church to help him or her continue moving toward the next stage of development.

- The primary barrier he or she faces that must be overcome to continue forward movement toward a deeper relationship with God.

- The primary ministry that can have a significant and positive impact on the traveler.

Remember that the job of the church is to place emphasis on the creation, ongoing maintenance and improvement of these ministries in order to have maximum impact in the life transforming process of discipleship.

As we said in chapter seven, the discipleship pathway is a map that can be used to put in place in the proper sequential order the ministries at each of the six stages of spiritual development that you learned about through the ocean diagram. This is not the latest, greatest, pre-packaged "program" that will turn your congregation into an Acts 2 church in ten easy steps. It is a template to use as a guide for the development of your own discipleship system. No two pathways are exactly alike, and each reflects the character of the church in which it is applied. The common denominator is that they all offer ministries that meet the needs of individuals at each of the six stages of spiritual development.

We interact with many pastors one-on-one, in teams with staff and lay leaders from their congregations, as well as a small group of pastors that meets weekly at the church where we work. Once they understand the concept of the ocean diagram and each of the steps on the discipleship pathway template, they retrace their steps and get back to the original ministry road where they started. They then begin thinking through what it actually takes to reach the destination they envision. Throughout the process, they assess and judge what they've done in the past, throw out what is no longer valid in light of this new information, and discover where their best ideas and strategies might actually fit in the context of making disciples.

The process of taking your church from where it is today to the point where you are ready to effectively lead your people into deeper spiritual water follows a critical path. Rather than walk in circles, hoping to figure out which turn to make and which hill to climb, the critical path will move you toward the implementation of a well-designed discipleship pathway.

Follow the Critical Path

First: Identify the Target

The purpose and goal of every local church congregation is to make disciples of Jesus. To accomplish the goal, you must first identify the target. A target is identified when the senior pastor wrestles with and answers the question, "What does a fully committed follower of Jesus Christ look like as a result of being discipled in my church?" This is not a question that can be answered by committee or group consensus. If the pastor is actively (or tacitly) leading one direction and the laity is attempting to go another, the result is a congregation that is lost in the woods, walking in circles, never reaching the destination.

The necessity of knowing and establishing a target can be found in a study of Moses as he leads the Israelites to the Promised Land. Moses had a clear target in mind. God gave him a vision, he knew exactly where he was going and where to lead his people. The power of that vision allowed him to prevail against the strangling grip of Pharaoh. It caused him to remain unflinching when he encountered the obstacle of the Red Sea. It sustained him when his community was in the middle of the desert with no food or water. Moses knew his target and he led the people toward it without compromise.

Moses remained on course until the spies he sent across the Jordan returned with a report that the land was impossible to conquer. Instead of remaining focused on God's purpose, he gave in to the consensus vote of a committee and immediately began walking in circles, lost in the woods (or, in his case, the desert) for the next forty years. Moses became an aimless leader. He still possessed amazing leadership skills, but for all intents and purposes, he no longer moved in the direction of the target. A pastor's personal theology of spiritual formation—"What does a fully committed follower look like?"—is the Promised Land. Knowing it and speaking it is the only way to identify the targeted destination toward which the congregation must move.

To answer the question, "What does a fully committed follower look like?" a pastor must do some significant soul searching. It will take long hours early in the morning and late at night, pouring over scripture. It will require a pastor to put his or her findings in front of trusted colleagues and have them critique it for flaws in his thinking. It will take months to develop a response that accurately reflects what personal believes. Without sweating over scripture passages, laying awake thinking through the meaning, and looking for their relevance to the process of spiritual development, a pastor is destined to sway back and forth in search of the next great idea coming down the pike.

There are some who have already answered the question "What does a fully committed follower of Jesus Christ look like as a result of being discipled in my church?" Mike Slaughter, senior pastor of Ginghamsburg Church, penned his answer in *Spiritual Entrepreneurs*. Bill Hybels upholds the Five Gs adopted by Willow Creek Community Church. We believe most senior pastors know deep inside what a fully committed follower ought to be. They may never have thought it through or put it on paper, and few have taken time to understand the importance of that theology to the effectiveness of their church. It is critical. A clearly articulated theology of spiritual development identifies and establishes the target toward which all ministries of the church must aim if the community of believers is going to reach its desired destination of becoming fully committed followers of Jesus.

Second: Partner for Success

The Role and Responsibility of the Visionary

The primary role of a senior pastor in every church of any size, whether a new church plant or an established congregation, is vision caster and culture changer. No one else can make that happen. As the pastor goes, so goes the church. That means the church will move forward if the pastor is leading the way. It also means the church will flounder if the pastor is lost in the spiritual woods and continues to walk in circles. For real forward movement to take place, the senior pastor must be a stage five or stage six follower. Remember, people become stage six followers by choice, not by accident. Each of us has the option to choose.

Like me, most pastors are big picture people. I believe God intended us to be that way because pastors are charged with leading the people by faith in Jesus into an invisible future. But being a visionary can be both a blessing and a curse for the church. The blessing is that big picture visionaries can see the potential future for their congregations, what the church can become and accomplish in the name of Jesus. They can see it so clearly they are able to describe it in word-pictures people understand and, suddenly, others are able to see it, too. They can build excitement and momentum as they passionately describe the future that lies ahead.

The curse, however, is that big picture people usually have a limited ability to translate that vision into a simple process and see the critical details that will allow for effective, quality implementation. Whether in the church or in the marketplace, visionaries typically know just enough about details and implementation to get something started then limp along. They often don't see the significant connections and bridges that must be built between the culture of the church, the internal structures that allow ministry to take place, and the implementation of effective ministry offerings.

Because detail work is more structured and less free flowing, it is often tedious and restrictive to a visionary. Therefore, they tend to mentally put details on the back burner. While visionaries see far ahead of today, they tend to live in the moment. Those things that were put on the back burner suddenly come to mind when the moment arrives in which they become relevant. Visionaries often find themselves caught off guard and too late to address an important detail. When a visionary is expected to be an implementer, many well-intentioned efforts are launched only to flounder or fail because the bases that are necessary for success were never covered.

These are not character flaws. These are merely the facts of visionary wiring. Detail work is not what visionaries do. We are not effective implementers. If you are a visionary pastor and no one has addressed this with you before, let me assure you that you are just what your church needs to become a place that makes disciples of all nations. However, you can sabotage yourself in one of two ways:

- You can refuse to move through your fear barrier, stay in your comfort zone and choose to walk in circles.

- You can refuse to delegate responsibility and authority for the detail work and partner with other followers you can trust to effectively implement your vision.

When I have a toothache and ask my dentist to correct the problem, I am entrusting him with the care of that tooth. I'm not asking him to schedule the appointment or mail me his invoice even though those things are important. I expect him to have others on his team to take care of those responsibilities. He might be able to accomplish those tasks, but only he can care for my tooth. That's his job. That's why he's in the position he is in. When I entrust a pastor with the spiritual leadership of my church, I expect that he or she will do the job and stay at the helm and do what only he or she can do. Ultimately, the endowment of the senior pastor within a congregation is keeper of the spiritual development process. It is not to do the hands-on ministry of which the staff and laity are capable.

I know where the church is and I have long been able to see the potential future when the lessons of the ocean diagram are applied. But it wasn't until I crossed paths with the person who became my ministry partner that I was finally able to begin developing a workable discipleship pathway that takes the philosophy and concepts of the ocean diagram and translates them into a map that can be used in the local church. Claudia Lavy and I have spent the past eight years pouring over the ocean diagram, assessing it, refining it, and sharing the message of it with as many people as possible.

Claudia was one of those teary-eyed people in the crowd. She caught and bought into the vision of the ocean diagram and has since made it her own. First and foremost, she's a disciple maker, but she's also a natural born detail-oriented implementer with the strength of connectedness[1]. As a visionary, I cannot implement as effectively without her help. As an implementer, she reminds me there is little to implement without the dreams of a visionary to begin with. Partners work together out of their individual strengths, and this is a team leadership model to which I encourage you, pastors in particular, to pay close attention if you are truly committed to building a vital, vibrant, disciple making church.

I have shared many of my personal stories with you through the ocean diagram. You will begin to hear many of Claudia's as well as you read the remaining chapters of this book. These are the implementation chapters, the "how to" that can help you create a discipleship pathway of your own.

THE ROLE AND RESPONSIBILITY OF THE IMPLEMENTER

While a pastor begins to establish a culture of intentional disciple making, he or she must also identify an implementer who is all of the following:

- A stage five or six follower;

- A disciple maker who is sold out to developing believers into followers (as opposed to an evangelist who has a passion for seeing unbelievers accept Christ);

- A process thinker who can make the connection between spiritual needs and what the church must offer to meet those needs;

- An organizational leader[2];

- A detail oriented implementer who places values on excellence and servanthood.

An implementer such as this can take the dreams of a visionary leader[3] and make them come true by partnering with him or her to build a discipleship pathway that revitalizes and transforms the church. We didn't say this person will be easy to find, but we know your implementer is out there. He or she will very likely have some

[1]Connectedness is defined in *Now, Discover Your Strengths* [Marcus Buckingham and Donald). Clinton (Free Press: New York, 2001)]
[2]Organizational leader is defined in *The Power of Team Leadership* (George Barna, 2001).
[3]Visionary leader is defined in *The Power of Team Leadership* (George Barna, 2001).

marketplace experience in which these skills have been used. However, we can't over emphasize the necessity for this person being a stage five or six follower who is sold out to a disciple making model of ministry, and not simply a person with nothing more than administrative or organizational skills from the marketplace. Many people can organize and administer details, but only a stage five or six follower of Christ who is sold out to discipleship will be able to make the necessary connections between the invisible spiritual needs of the people in your church and the ministries that are offered.

Take note that we said "partnering with" and not "doing for." The pastor must personally own the discipleship pathway because, as the pastor goes, so goes the church. It will be up to him or her to cast the vision of intentional discipleship and the value of participating in the journey along the discipleship pathway to the men and women of the congregation from the pulpit, in the newsletter, at board meetings, and anywhere there is an opportunity to do so. The pastor doesn't have to have intimate knowledge of **how** every piece is implemented, but it is absolutely necessary that the pastor knows and agrees with **what** is implemented, **why** it is being offered, and the quality and integrity of the presentation. If the pastor is not fully invested in it, he or she will not sell it. Instead, the pastor will talk about what a great concept it is and abdicate responsibility for driving the process. It will be left up to the staff or unpaid ministry leaders to develop and implement under their own power and they, left leaderless, will never produce a product that makes a significant impact.

Third: Design the Pathway

Once the target has been identified, the pastor takes the next step by developing a preliminary pathway concept. We have seen pathways in the shape of stars, circles, baseball diamonds, crosses, rivers, and even a rocket ship that launches into orbit! Again, the common denominator is that they all incorporate ministries that meet the needs of individuals at each of the six stages of spiritual development.

In the chapters that follow, we will offer objectives, criteria and measurements for each primary ministry to help you design the stepping-stones along your pathway.

- Objectives will identify the goal of each ministry.

- Criteria will provide examples against which each ministry can be compared to insure the purpose is being fulfilled.

- Measurements will assess the effectiveness of each ministry.

By placing the discipleship pathway over your current ministry offerings like a template, you will be able to:

- Identify existing ministries that meet the criteria for effectiveness;

- Identify areas that lack or are weak in ministries that address discipling needs;

- Identify ineffective ministries that do not address the discipling needs of people at any stage;

- Properly arrange ministries to meet needs at the appropriate stage of spiritual development.

- Measure the effectiveness of your ministries in moving people toward spiritual maturity.

What was once an array of unrelated, disconnected programs can be refined and organized into a clear, understandable pathway people are able to follow.

As you move through the design process, it will be necessary to make a ruthless assessment of your entire church, including worship, hospitality, facilities, classes, administration, groups, events, ministries for adults, youth and children, congregational care. Everything! You will have to look at each piece objectively as though you are seeing it for the first time. There can be no holding onto sacred cows if you want your church to be a haven of effective disciple making.

There are three areas the discipleship pathway does not directly address: congregational care, prayer, and leadership development. Each is an area of ministry that is crucial to the effectiveness of the entire church, and each must be carried out with the same excellence and quality you build into your discipling ministries.

For the purpose of this book, we must assume your church has or will establish and implement effective organizational and administrative structures to support the pathway you are about to develop. Organizational structures are the models you use to organize your leadership, manage your staff and ministry leaders, structure your small groups, etc. Administrative structures are the processes and procedures you establish to effectively conduct day-to-day business, such as communication processes, financial procedures, etc. Look to other progressive churches as well as the secular marketplace for policies, procedures, processes, and structures that have been successful and incorporate them into your church. To underscore the necessity of building a strong, supportive foundation upon which to build the pathway, here are a few resources we recommend:

- *How to Break Growth Barriers* [Carl George with Warren Bird (Baker Book House: Grand Rapids MI, 1993)];

- *The Power of Team Leadership* (George Barna, 2001);

- *Prepare Your Church for the Future* [Carl George (Baker Book House: Grand Rapids MI, 2000)];

- *Simply Strategic Stuff* [Tim Stevens and Tony Morgan (Group Publishing, Inc.: Loveland CO, 2004)];

- *Safe and secure: The Alban Guide to Protecting Your Congregation* (Jeffrey W. Hanna).

The church is desperately waiting for leaders to step to the forefront, own the truth that is preached from the pulpit, and put it into usable form without apology. This is the point at which most churches struggle because there does not exist a strong enough fire in the belly of the leaders to pursue something more. Their people are left to live out their days spiritually wasting away in their comfort zones. Too many pastors and church boards are driven by a need to be liked instead of being driven by a desire to build a disciple making environment that garners the respect of churched and unchurched alike. Power flows through a congregation whose senior pastor takes personal responsibility for the spiritual development of his or her people. Your people are waiting. Their emotion is real, their longing is deep, and their desire to see the church rise up and actually meet spiritual need is immense. Moving your church to the next level of effectiveness will upset some because their boats will be rocked. You and your implementers will be called pushy, demanding, and insensitive. It will take everything you've got to turn the tide. As we have partnered with God in turning around our church (a previously declining congregation established in the 1860s), we have often acknowledged why more churches don't do this. It is hard, sometimes unpopular work that doesn't seem urgent in comparison to the next hospital visit, funeral, or barrage of phone messages. And you must remain on constant watch to insure the integrity of each ministry is preserved.

But the rewards are there.

- A man serving as a senior pastor for twenty-three years said, "I feel like I can finally begin my ministry."

- A woman with great potential stayed in her husband's shadow, believing all she had to contribute was support for him. She now leads a hospitality and food service ministry that serves 600 people each week.

- A young wife and mother confused about God's call found her purpose as a teacher of a core class on the discipleship pathway. She helped write original curriculum, established a standard of excellence in teaching, then passed the baton to another as God began to move her to lead a women's discipling ministry.

There came a moment in the woods of West Virginia when I knew I had to do something different. I had to give up my clever idea, stop guessing, and move onto a path that would actually lead me home. Changing the direction in which your church is currently moving will take serious thought, hard work, and team leadership, but it will be the journey of a lifetime. With an understanding of the ocean diagram in our backpacks, let's take the next steps.

A Note to Professional Clergy

God speaks deeply into the heart of a pastor. There are many pastors who have never really heard from God in regard to leading a congregation into a deep and abiding relationship with Christ. Some may have had a spiritual awakening and read it as a call to pastoral ministry when, in fact, it was simply a profound moment in their personal transformation. It was never God's intention for them to assume pastoral leadership of a local church. This is a tough but critical issue that must be addressed as a church prepares to become a disciple making environment.

Churches suffering the consequences of aimless wandering can always trace the problem back to lack of leadership by the senior pastor. Either he was never supposed to be a pastoral leader or she has made incorrect leadership choices. To move a congregation forward, the pastor of a plateaued or declining church must know whether he or she is truly called to lead a local congregation. If so, he or she must also make the necessary choices to lead people toward becoming fully committed followers. The ability of your church to revitalize depends on this. As the pastor goes, so goes the church.

A Note to District and Conference Level Leaders

An annual conference[4] is the "local church" and the bishop is the "local pastor" to his or her district superintendents. The district[5] is the "local church" and the district superintendent is the "local pastor" to the pastors he or she supervises. Every lesson from the ocean diagram can be applied to an annual conference or a district. Meetings, events, and gatherings should be worth the time and energy of the participants to come and see. Those participants should find their expectations exceeded by authentic, high impact hospitality when they arrive. If those participants feel the efforts of the district or the conference are irrelevant to the reality of local church life, each will arrive in a state of heightened sensitivity. "The conference? Can any thing good come from there?" they cynically ask. You can prove everything good can come from there and win their hearts for the mission by applying each lesson to your particular context. If district and conference leaders begin to do whatever it takes to minister to their "congregations", set the expectation and be the example, then hold their pastors accountable for doing the same, there will not be enough buildings to contain us.

[4]In the United Methodist Church, an annual conference is an organizational structure, a geographical area and a periodic meeting of clergy and elected lay members.
[5]A district is a division of the annual conference and serves as a link between the local church and the conference.

CHAPTER NINE

Invitational Discipleship

A Note To Professional Clergy

Transforming your church into a haven of life transformation begins with the senior pastor casting a vision of intentional discipleship. This initial vision should be cast over a period of many months, first to your most trusted "inner circle" influencers, then to your elders or leadership board, then to your staff, and finally to your congregation. You must answer the questions, calm the fears, and expand the vision of all those to whom you speak in order to generate buy-in and support for the changes that will take place. The process of casting your vision should be slow, deliberate, carefully thought through, and strategically designed. It first should be couched in non-threatening language and "what if" terms, first, ("What if we designed a pathway that would help our church fulfill the Great Commission?") long before it is spoken of in terms of "we're going to." Establish a biblical foundation for the vision then, when the time is right, begin presenting it from the pulpit, in the newsletter, and through all-church mailings. It should present a word-picture of an appealing and desired future. Will you have full support? No. Will the majority buy in to the vision? Yes. Will you lose some people along the way? Probably. There are those who will immediately catch the vision and make it their own. The majority will not resist and will buy into the vision a bit less quickly than the more visionary early adopters. A few will grumble and wait to see if it is actually going to work before they climb onboard. Then there are the arsonists who will never adopt the vision but instead will try burning it to the ground at every turn. You will need to prepare yourself physically, mentally, and most of all, spiritually for the road ahead because the ride will be rough in spots along the way. But, like anyone hoping to reap a harvest, the ground must first be prepared. Now is the time to pull out all the stops on your vision casting skills. You will need them over the next four to five years as your discipleship pathway evolves from concept to reality.

You read that correctly. Four to five years is the approximate time frame for developing and fully implementing a pathway. It took us four and a half years from the time we first developed the concept of the pathway to the time we put the final piece in place. There are parts of the process you will launch and absolutely hate once you see them in action. So it's back to the drawing board to redesign and try again. We totally overhauled orientation four times before we found an effective format. We adjusted the time slots we chose for classes, changed and rewrote curriculum, watched facilitators come and go, adjusted tracking systems, and needed time to recruit the right servants. There is a lot of work to do to become effective at making disciples. Remember, the discipleship pathway is not a program and it does not offer a quick fix. It's a map to follow to align your church with the process of discipleship that is a spiritual reality taking place all around us every single day, whether we cooperate with it or not. If you embark on a journey to become a disciple making church, you will need to commit to the long haul and be prepared to cast your vision, as Buzz Lightyear would say, "To infinity and beyond!"

Give Me a Reason to Return

Darren had not been in church for thirty years. The discovery of throat cancer shook him to the core as he came face to face with his own mortality. Like so many in similar life-threatening situations, he decided to get back into church and seek God's mercy and rescue. He was extremely hesitant to do so, however, because he was a recovering alcoholic, a "sinner", and everyone in the community knew him. Who would want him to walk through the doors of their church? A friend invited Darren's wife to church and she asked him to go along. After a great deal of thought and conversation with his wife, he finally mustered the courage to give it a try. Much to his surprise, several people he had known for many years greeted and welcomed him with open arms. In fact, Darren felt so accepted he decided to return the following Sunday.

Allen was as far from the church as anyone could possibly be. He had been in both legal and financial trouble and was as emotionally low as he could get. He knew he couldn't climb out of his hopelessness without connecting with God. He had brushed against the church as a child, mostly attending Christmas and Easter services with his aunt, but those experiences left memories of sermons that had nothing to do with reality and music he could painfully endure at best. Allen would never dream of listening to that outside the sanctuary of a church. How do you connect with God when you're bored to death by the very place that claims to have the answer? Several friends told him about a church that played the same type music he loved to listen to on the radio. Supposedly, this church also had a preacher who spoke in plain language about topics that really hit home. He decided to give it a try. The following Sunday, Allen arrived apprehensive about what he would find. He could see the greeters at the door as he approached the church, and nervously wondered if the jeans and tee shirt he was wearing would be out of place. He was relieved when they greeted him warmly. They seemed genuinely glad to see him. As he moved into the lobby, Allen found a table beautifully decorated with linens and a floral centerpiece. It was piled high with trays of homemade cookies. Next to it was another linen covered table that held carafes of regular and decaf coffee, as well as lemonade. Allen thought, "Wow! This is really nice!" When the music and the message turned out to be meaningful as well, he decided to return the following Sunday.

Alex and Bethany were a thirtysomething couple. Alex grew up in a Christian home, was educated in a Christian school, and had attended church his entire life. Bethany became a Christian as an adult and had served a church in children's ministry for several years. She had been worked to death there and the leadership was disconnected from and insensitive to the servants who actually made ministry happen. To make matters worse, what was preached from the pulpit and lived out in real life did not match. As a result, Alex and Bethany lost trust in the leadership and began searching for a new church home. One Sunday morning, they stopped by a church some friends attended and tried out an adult Sunday school class. One man spoke openly about his struggle with alcohol. Alex and Bethany were shocked, but as they scanned the other faces in the room, no one seemed rattled by his confession. When class ended they stayed for worship and found it filled with great music and a sermon that addressed issues they were currently facing. Bethany commented on the way home, "I loved worship, but I don't think I want to go to a church that has alcoholics in the congregation." After further conversation, however, she and Alex both realized a church where people speak truthfully about their failures and shortcomings is exactly the type of church they were looking for. They decided to return the following Sunday.

All of these people have three things in common: an old trusted friend or family member who talked about the church in a way that caused each person to become curious enough to visit, they had an experience that overcame their heightened sensitivity, and they encountered music and a message that was relevant to their lives. As a result, each decided to return the following Sunday.

Invitational Discipleship

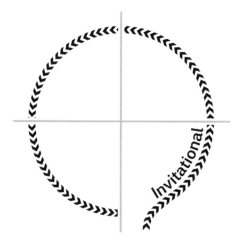

Intentional invitational discipleship creates a culture in which the people of your church contagiously extend invitations to their unchurched friends and family, and then receive them as welcome, expected guests for whom the church has prepared itself. Creating such a culture starts with the core leadership of the church making a commitment to offer nothing but culturally relevant, well-produced ministry. They understand that doing anything less erodes the ability of the church to transform lives.

This first section of the discipleship pathway is devoted to discipling the cynical unchurched people at stage one, and the highly sensitized people at stage two who are curious enough about God and the church they heard about from their friends or family to actually visit.

Come and See: Worship Worth Experiencing

A come and see ministry is so attractive and carried out with such excellence that the people of your congregation will stake their reputation in the marketplace on it, and will not hesitate to invite unchurched friends and family.

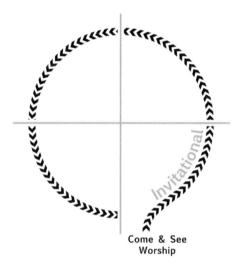

Come & See
Worship

Ultimately, every ministry of the church should be worth coming and seeing, but the development of a discipleship pathway begins with a primary path for adults to follow. As the pathway is developed and implemented, it will begin to create a culture of intentionality that spreads to other discipling ministries such as youth and children's ministries. Elements of the pathway, particularly come and see and authentic high impact hospitality, will begin to influence and transform every other ministry in your church. As you raise the bar on relevance and excellence, you will discover that the people of your congregation will rise to these new expectations.

In the development of a pathway for adult discipleship, we must start at the widest point of entry: worship. While some may enter through a small group, a class, or the annual church picnic, worship continues to serve as the main door into the life of the church and is therefore the first step on the discipleship pathway. That means it is the first area of ministry that must be assessed with brutal honesty and be transformed into an experience worth coming and seeing. In workshops around the country, we have asked pastors, "Now that you've heard the ocean diagram and the discipleship pathway, on what area do you plan to put your initial focus?" Most immediately move to hospitality, classes, or small groups, and completely sidestep come and see worship. By their own admission, pastors say that pride keeps them from wanting to take a long, hard look at the quality of their worship because a brutally honest assessment might reveal an experience that's really not worth coming and seeing after all. That's not only painful, but it's also personal. Worship is the one area of ministry over which the pastor has the most control and input. It's also complicated. There are multiple components to worship, including musicians, singers, ushers, greeters, liturgists, bulletins, sound, lighting, media, etc. The sheer number of people involved in making worship happen can be overwhelming. Nevertheless, a come and see worship experience is the first step on an effective discipleship pathway and must be the step that is developed first. Designing a pathway that skips over this crucial first step will create a riverbed that remains dry. Dazzling hospitality, a dynamite orientation, and powerful giving and receiving ministries are of limited value if there are no visitors feeding the flow of people that move through your pathway. Remember, you cannot measure the effectiveness of your worship by counting those who are already committed to the church. Churched people who have made an emotional investment in your congregation will come to virtually anything the church offers. The acid test of an effective come and see worship experience is whether or not your average attendee will stake his or her personal reputation among unchurched friends and family on the quality of your worship experience and actually invite them.

The objective of a come and see ministry is to offer a culturally relevant experience that compels parishioners to invite their unchurched friends and family and draws unchurched people into the life of the church. When worship builds a bridge between the church and the culture, old-trusted friends like Philip naturally begin to invite their unchurched and disconnected friends like Nathaniel. When the "old trusted friends" sitting in your pews are engaged in the excitement and energy created by a come and see worship experience, they will be compelled to talk about it. They will either directly invite others, or create curiosity by the enthusiasm conveyed through their conversation.

The *Megachurches Today 2005* research study by Leadership Network and the Hartford Institute for Religion Research states, "Megachurches grow because excited attendees tell their friends." Whether yours is a small, medium, or large church, cynicism is replaced by curiosity, and people show up to see what the hubbub is all about when you intentionally offer a worship experience worth coming and seeing.

We earlier defined a come and see ministry as one that "is so attractive and carried out with such excellence that the people of your congregation will stake their reputation in the marketplace on it and will not hesitate to invite unchurched friends and family." The Merriam Webster dictionary defines attractive as "arousing interest". To explore that meaning a bit further, the definition of arousing is "to awaken from sleep; to rouse or stimulate to action." These words have potent spiritual implications, both for the people in your pews and the unchurched people who visit. An attractive worship experience is more than a seamless stage presentation; it has the potential to rouse or stimulate parishioners to take action and invite their unchurched friends and family. It also has the potential to awaken unchurched people from their spiritual slumber and motivate them to act on their newfound spiritual curiosity. Of course it is God's prevenient grace that paves the way, but the role of the church is to work in harmony with God and create an environment conducive to such an experience.

Excellence is defined as "first class; of the highest quality." Excellence in ministry happens when the leadership is uncompromising in its commitment to high quality. In the context of worship, it means the music is comparable to what people listen to outside the church. It means professional quality media, sound, lighting, stage decoration, print, and electronic images. It means ushers and greeters are trained and attentive, verbal announcements are strategically planned and presented by an articulate announcer, baptisms and the receiving of new members are thoughtfully incorporated into the order and flow of worship. It means worship is presented in unique, exciting, and unexpected ways without distractions.

Creating a come and see worship experience requires an understanding of several key elements.

The Target Audience

Who are you trying to reach? Is it families with elementary age children; retiree "snowbirds" who winter in your Sunbelt community; young adult couples with or without infants and toddlers; middle age empty nesters? It will take demographic and ethnographic research to help identify your target audience. You can obtain information through many sources, including the U.S. Census Bureau, your local Chamber of Commerce, and possibly through your denominational headquarters.

The Felt Needs of the Target Audience

Once you determine whom you are trying to reach, you are then in a position to research and determine felt needs. In other words, what are their unaddressed emotional longings? Parents of young children may long for a safe, secure nursery that allows them to relax during worship. Seniors may long for familiar hymns and logical expository preaching. Young adults may long to experience God through introspective music, atmospheric lighting, and visual arts. One large 3,500-attendance church conducted focus groups to identify the felt needs of its target audience. They gathered together small groups of people who exemplified the target and asked them questions that revealed their thoughts and ideas about an ideal worship experience. You can also canvas the neighborhood with door-to-door surveys, or simply be intentional about talking with both churched and unchurched people in regard to their needs, then compile your findings. You run the risk of missing the mark entirely if you guess at felt needs, so do the homework and find the true needs of the people you intend to attract.

Determining felt needs will not only pay off as you design a relevant worship experience, but will also provide data to create an overall church experience that meets needs beyond worship. You will discover needs specific to your targeted group, such as opportunities for seniors to fellowship together, support groups for people in recovery from illness, addictions, or grief, play groups for parents of toddlers, progressive student and children's ministries that connect kids to God and mature them in their faith, etc.

What It Takes to Make Worship Culturally Relevant

Relevant worship differs by age, stage of life, lifestyle, culture, etc. It's not difficult to educate yourself about culturally relevant worship for both your existing congregation and the unchurched group you target, but it takes time and effort. There is a multitude of books, publications, and websites that can enlighten you to the endless possibilities. There are also seminars, workshops, and conferences offered practically year round by churches all over the United States that currently produce effective, relevant worship that attracts a broad spectrum of individuals. These are learning tools that can equip you with an understanding of how to create worship that appeals to your particular target audience.

While elements of relevant worship differ among target audiences, there are two fundamental components that must be effectively developed in all styles of worship - preaching and music. It doesn't matter if you've addressed everything else if the audience is not able to connect with the music or the message.

Preaching

Not every pastor is born to be a great preacher, but it is possible to improve preaching skills through reading books, listening to audio recordings of effective, high quality preachers and studying their techniques, or having a respected colleague preview your sermon and offer constructive feedback. We know one pastor who obtains DVDs and transcripts of sermons from preachers recognized nationally for their speaking abilities like Mike Slaughter, Bill Hybels, Rick Warren, Tony Evans, and Kirby John Caldwell, practices writing sermons that are similar in style, and incorporates elements of their delivery that are compatible with his personality into his own presentations.

To truly make an impact, a sermon must:

- Be inspired by the Holy Spirit. That means studying the Word and seeking God's direction and guidance well in advance;

- Address topics and make points people can relate to their own lives;

- Interpret scripture. That means taking the Word and making a connection through real life stories and examples with which the audience can identify;

- Contain humor that puts people at ease;

- Be offered in common language people understand;

- Contain action steps for people to follow;

- Be presented in multi-sensory ways to reach people at all levels of learning.

Dallas Willard, former pastor and now philosophy professor at the University of Southern California, said in an interview with Christianity Today, "We have a lot of talk about grace but when you look at the concrete form that it takes in institutional life, it's legalism. And it's backbreaking, and it's not good news."[1] Too often grace is a detached abstract theological concept, some arrangement in heaven called 'unmerited favor.' Where you need unmerited favor is at street level. When we communicate to people at street level, create disparity between what their life is and what it can be through Jesus Christ, and show them a picture of a preferred future, they not only return the following week ready to hear more, but they also begin to respond to the call of God to move toward deeper spiritual water.

MUSIC

Connecting with God through music is central to conveying the gospel in a meaningful way. Eighteen to thirty-five year olds will not relate to the same music as thirty-five to fifty year olds. Young adults in a major metropolitan urban setting will not relate to the same music as young adults in a rural mid-western county seat. In the course of your target audience research, you will discover the style of music that can create a connection between people and the Holy Spirit. Charles Wesley understood this concept when he put Christian lyrics to the music of drinking songs so unchurched people who hung out in the pubs of England could relate to the church. All music becomes sacred when it connects people with God.

Finding musicians to play quality music is always a challenge, especially for small and mid-size congregations, but it is not beyond the realm of possibility to develop a high quality music ministry that can compete with music offered by the culture. The key is effective networking. Ask around among the people of your church. "Do you know anyone who is a really good musician?" "Who do you know that has a great voice?" You may find excellent musicians and vocalists right in your own pews, but don't limit your search. Look outside the walls of

---

[1]*Measuring What Matters* A LEADERSHIP Forum, Leadership Journal, Spring 2000.

your church into the community as well. There are excellent musicians who play in local restaurants and bars that may be more than willing to either launch a band for your church, or actually become part of your band and make the church their own. The senior pastor at the church where we work is a top-notch networker. After swimming laps at the local YMCA, he moves into the hot tub where he strikes up conversations with people from all walks of life. Bill's "hot tub ministry" has resulted not only in numerous people coming to our church, sometimes for the first time in their lives, but it also is a source of knowledge about great local musicians.

As you search for musicians, be alert and ready to find them in unexpected places. A woman who attended our church offered to paint murals on the walls of the preschool classrooms and she brought her brother along to help. Our pastor struck up a conversation with the young man and discovered that Brian was not attending church, he was a draftsman for a greenhouse manufacturer, and he was a drummer who had played professionally. Bill told him we were thinking of forming a band that played alternative music and wondered if he might be interested in helping it get off the ground. Brian found that idea very appealing and has been part of the band for over four years. He and his wife are growing Christians who are actively connected to a small group, and their children have both attended our preschool. High quality musicians and vocalists are out there, but you have to be committed to the search and intentional about finding them.

As you identify your audience, develop an understanding of the felt needs, and begin to align your current worship experience with the objective, all of your ideas and plans must be filtered through the criteria for establishing a come and see worship experience. Does this experience overcome the cynicism of the unchurched person and the hesitation of parishioners to invite unchurched people? When you can honestly answer yes, you are moving toward new life in your congregation.

Once you've launched your new and improved worship experience, how do you know if you've hit the mark? The only way to determine if anything you attempt is successful is to measure the results. In the area of come and see worship, effectiveness is quantifiable and is measured by the number of first time visitors. You might collect that information by using attendance pads with a column for first time visitors or bulletins with a tear off stub for them to fill out and drop in the offering plate. There are numerous methods to use. Once it is collected, however, a good database is crucial to gauging effectiveness of ministry, not only at this stage, but also of ministry that targets people at the second stage of spiritual development—authentic high impact hospitality.

Objective of come and see: To offer a culturally relevant experience that compels parishioners to invite their unchurched friends and family and draws the unchurched person into the life of the church.
Criteria for come and see: Does this experience overcome the cynicism of the unchurched person and the hesitation of parishioners to invite unchurched people?
Measurement of effectiveness: The number of first time visitors

Authentic High Impact Hospitality

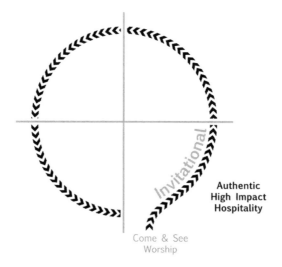

Authentic high impact hospitality exceeds the expectations of curious visitors, creates a WOW experience, and causes them to feel both welcome and expected.

You've raised the bar for worship and your people have begun inviting others. Curious stage two friends and family members have believed their old-trusted friends, just as the Samaritan townspeople believed the woman who met Jesus at the well, and they are cautiously approaching the doors of your church. Their cynicism is still in tact and the heightened sensitivity that began growing the moment they accepted the invitation is compounding their fears. They are filled with that anxious, queasy feeling we all get when we find ourselves in unknown territory. The responsibility of the church is to address and help them overcome both the cynicism and the heightened sensitivity in those first crucial moments when visitors arrive. Authentic high impact hospitality is the ministry that can put them at ease and clear the way to move forward in their spiritual journey.

Authenticity

To make a transforming difference, authenticity cannot be the designated responsibility of one ministry. It is a culture that must be created and permeate the entire church family. Authenticity among the ranks always begins with the senior pastor and senior leadership staff. Their ability and willingness to self-disclose creates an openness and honesty that sets an example to follow. Men and women in senior leadership must be willing to see themselves as others see them, courageously face and acknowledge their shortcomings, and set an example of lifelong learning and personal growth. In doing so, there will begin a snowball effect among the staff and lay leadership. Everyone begins to relax about personal flaws and foibles, and becomes empowered to actually work on overcoming self-defeating behaviors. In the beginning of this chapter, Alex and Bethany thought long and hard about attending a church where a man talked openly about his alcoholism before coming to the conclusion that they were experiencing a church filled with authentic people. Authenticity conveys grace and hope. Ken Fong, senior pastor of Evergreen Baptist Church in Rosemead, California explained in an interview with Christianity Today that he conveys the message this way, "There are two parts of the Good News. First, everyone's a rat. Only when you know you're a rat are you ready for the second part: God is not an exterminator."[2] Authenticity, combined with relevant worship, brings seekers of grace and hope back to your church where they have the opportunity to connect with God.

Authenticity must be interpreted as well as demonstrated. In the larger context of the church family, a vision of authentic hospitality must be cast from the pulpit. People need to understand the benefits of authenticity. While everyone has personally encountered a phony,

[2]*Measuring What Matters* A LEADERSHIP Forum, Leadership Journal, Spring 2000.

inauthentic greeting, they will personally begin to change their behavior when they are repeatedly reminded of the discomfort of their own experience, shown how Jesus set a different example, and challenged to go beyond phoniness to authenticity. In the smaller context of frontline hospitality ministries, "why" training begins to change the culture among those who serve. Obviously, servants in every area of ministry must be trained in the "how to" of their jobs. "Why" training helps them understand how they fit into the larger mission and vision of the church, and how they personally participate in the making of disciples. A two-step model of training that includes both why and how looks like this:

1. Why?

   Servants need to know why this church bothers to do the task of the ministry to which they have committed to serve. By walking them through the ocean diagram and explaining the stages of spiritual development up to the stage their ministry targets, they begin to see the larger picture of God's plan for life transformation. As they understand the primary person and primary barrier at each stage, they begin to understand why they are asked to do the task before them. They understand both the target and the goal of their ministry and become better equipped to serve. For example, when a servant who bakes cookies for Sunday morning refreshments understands the process of spiritual development, that servant becomes more committed to the overall mission of the church. Homemade cookies and a cup of coffee help a curious visitor feel welcome and invited. When they feel welcome and invited, they begin to overcome their heightened sensitivity. When their sensitivities decrease, they will have a more positive experience and want to return. When they return, they will have the opportunity to hear the gospel and accept Christ. Did the cookie baker lead that person into a personal relationship with Christ? Indirectly, by providing a means to overcome the barrier that had the potential to stop that person dead in his or her tracks. We tell our cookie bakers, "Don't ever let us catch you saying, 'Oh, I'm just a cookie baker.' Your contribution is of great value, and your role is critical to the effectiveness of the discipleship pathway!" Each servant is empowered when they understand how he or she fits into the bigger plan.

2. How?

Once servants are trained in the "why" of their job, the way has been paved for the ministry's leadership to train them in the "how to" of their particular assignment.

Authenticity demonstrated by senior leaders, vision cast from the pulpit, and training focused on why each ministry is important to life transformation changes the culture of a church to one that is saturated with authenticity. A church that lacks this invisible quality at the upper-most levels of leadership will experience only puddles of authenticity here and there, while a river of inauthentic ministry continues to flow. On the other hand, a river flowing with authenticity leaves behind only isolated puddles of phony behavior. But even those stuck in the puddles will benefit by the grace that bubbles up in a culture of authenticity.

High Impact Hospitality

Every church has some form of hospitality, even if nothing more than a lukewarm usher who doles out bulletins at the entrance to the sanctuary. What we're calling for is *high impact* hospitality. You can walk into most any establishment and be treated hospitably, but rarely encounter a situation where you actually say, "WOW! This is more than I expected! These people have gone out of their way to make me feel welcome. It's obvious they actually thought about my needs in advance!"

Bear in mind that we are not competing with other churches in our quest to capture the hearts of unchurched people. We are competing with the culture. When the greeter at Wal-Mart makes people feel more welcome than the greeter at church, we're not doing our job. When the restrooms at the local family restaurant are cleaner than the restrooms at church, we are not doing our job. When kids are more captivated by the activities sponsored by the city parks department than by the activities in the children's ministry, and adults find greater relevance in Sunday morning political television talk shows than in worship, we are not doing our job. The commitment of leadership to excellence must go beyond come and see worship into all areas of ministry. Once again, the attractiveness of what is offered has the power to awaken people from their spiritual slumber.

To create a culture of high impact hospitality, everything that leaves a first impression must be aligned with the objective, which is to create an environment that will encourage the curious visitor to return. There are eight major areas that require evaluation with the same brutal honesty with which worship was assessed.

- Facilities;

- Parking;

- Greeters and ushers;

- Refreshments;

- Signage;

- Bulletins & announcements;

- Childcare;

- Visitor follow up.

Look at each area through the eyes of a stranger. Better yet, ask someone you trust who does not attend your church and who possesses strong evaluation skills to make an honest assessment. Based on your findings, the task at hand will be to improve, upgrade, and, in some instances, create new ministries. Each idea and plan should be filtered through the criteria for authentic high impact hospitality. Does this experience overcome the heightened sensitivity of the curious visitor? With the objective and criteria in mind, let's look at each of these eight areas.

FACILITIES: THE EXTERIOR

The first impression made by your church begins at the curb. Is the parking lot well maintained, or full of potholes? Is the lawn manicured? Are the shrub beds weeded and mulched? Did the last servant who worked outside leave the hose lying on the ground? Do the plastic pots by the front door still have dead mums in them from last fall? Is the exterior of the building well maintained, or is the paint peeling? We know of one church that actually located a dumpster next to the front door of its new $1.5 million addition because it provided convenient access to the people of the church. High impact hospitality that overcomes the heightened sensitivity of curious visitors means the dumpster moves to a less conspicuous location, and the church family bites the bullet and walks a bit farther. Red flags of caution would pop up in our minds if you or I entered an establishment with an unattractive, poorly maintained exterior. Those same red flags are raised in the minds of the people you are targeting when the unattractive, poorly maintained exterior belongs to your church.

FACILITIES: THE INTERIOR

What do we do when we invite guests to our homes? We clean house! A few dishes in the sink, a couple of unmade beds, and stacks of unopened mail aren't a concern unless company's coming. Then we clean surfaces we don't otherwise notice! When the church family begins inviting guests, the house needs to be cleaned up. High impact hospitality greets guests with a clean, orderly, uncluttered facility.

A pastor newly appointed to a 120-attendance church was thrilled when friends from his former church showed up for worship and Sunday school one weekend. But he was then humiliated when they reported to him hey noticed a pile of dried up, rock-hard dog feces in the corner of a classroom. No one had bothered to clean it up for God only knows how long. Or maybe they hadn't noticed it tucked up against the piles of old, unused hymnals stacked along the wall. We walk through churches all over the country and constantly encounter lobbies lined with tables cluttered with unmatched gloves left in the sanctuary the previous Sunday and leftover dishes from the last carry-in dinner owners never bothered to retrieve; bulletin boards crammed with notices from local civic organizations that no one reads but we are too polite to throw away; empty display racks no one bothers to refill. These are the first impressions we create for first time visitors.

If you have not already taken the initiative to clean out the "sacred junk" that fills every nook and cranny of your church building, please consider this permission to do so. Heightened sensitivity is only increased when cluttered spaces create an environment more like a storage closet than a lobby, sanctuary, or classroom. Clutter turns people away and interferes with the mission of the church. We have to move our commitment away from personal agendas that would have us cling to unused, worthless items and toward the mission of Christ. That is not to say we should blindly discard everything we encounter. Instead, find someone in the church family who has attended long enough to know the history of the church and its people, and who has also bought into the vision of revitalization. Check with that person about any item you suspect may hold sentimental value before you decide how to dispose of it. You may need to return some items to the original donor, or get their permission to sell or give it away. You may make some items such as unused furniture available for sale to the church family. Many will be thrilled to have a piece of history. For the most part, however, churches are clogged with unnecessary and unusable leftovers from past events, classes, and groups, as well as outdated office supplies that should simply be thrown away. By all means do it!

As you assess, also look closely at the quality of housekeeping. Are glass entry doors covered with fingerprints? Are the carpets cleaned and swept, or are they covered with stains and debris? Are hard floors mopped and polished? Are the restrooms clean, well ventilated, and stocked with paper products? Do you find cobwebs in the corners and dust on horizontal surfaces? Are classroom tabletops covered with dried glue from a craft project, or are they ready for a guest to use for the very first time? Does the custodial staff make sure tables, chairs, and equipment are returned to a state of readiness, or are they left askew after being used? The facility is to the church what a model home is to a builder. It showcases who we are and what we value. High impact hospitality means we clean up the church just like we clean up our homes when we are expecting company. The difference is the church never knows when guests will drop by so it must *always* be ready for visitors, just like a model home.

PARKING

The frustration of trying to find a place at a strange location that does not have ample parking has the potential to drive visitors away. They will simply go home or go elsewhere. If you are fortunate enough to have a newer facility, you more than likely have adequate parking. Many older churches are parking space challenged and may not have the physical ability to increase the number of spaces. In those situations, it's time to get creative. Set an expectation that staff and ministry leaders park further away to make space close to the church available for visitors. Contact nearby businesses that are closed during your worship times and ask permission to use their parking lots, and then publicize these new parking options in your bulletin. In the course of casting a vision of attracting the unchurched, encourage regular attendees to take advantage of these new options to free up space for visitors.

Consider all your alternatives and come up with ways to increase parking and make it more convenient for your guests.

GREETERS AND USHERS

When you create a culture of authenticity, greeters and ushers will demonstrate that quality to curious stage two visitors. There are numerous resources available that can help you up the quality and type of service provided by greeters and ushers. You must decide what best fits into your vision. It might be greeters in the parking lot as well as the front door; information and welcome desk servants; hosts and hostesses in the children's ministry, nursery and classrooms. Wherever you strategically place them, authenticity is the overarching quality they must convey.

To exceed a visitor's expectations, ushers and greeters must go beyond the obligatory handshake, "Good morning!" and a bulletin. They must anticipate and proactively meet the needs of the people they encounter. High impact hospitality means they don't merely point in the direction of the nursery, it means they escort a guest to the nursery. It means they don't tell guests who arrive to a packed house that's already standing and singing that there are seats over there toward the front of the worship area. It means they go find empty seats, return, retrieve the guests and escort them to those seats. Does someone look lost or confused? Ushers and greeters should be expected to watch for those indicators and ask if they can help . . . then actually help!

Fellowship Bible Church in Little Rock, Arkansas has reserved a section of their parking lot close to the main entrance for first time visitors. As guests arrive, a parking lot attendant introduces himself and asks their names. After a brief conversation, the greeter sends them off in the direction of the entrance then contacts the greeters stationed at the entrance doors via walkie-talkie with the name of each guest. Can't you hear the surprised, "WOW!" when guests are welcomed by name?

REFRESHMENTS

Have you noticed that even a 400-pound man can feel more secure behind a cup of coffee! When we greet guests in our own homes, we offer them something to eat or drink to make them feel welcome and put them at ease. The rationale behind offering refreshments when guests first enter the church is the same.

A 350-attendance church had limited lobby space, so they offered refreshments in the social hall that was located in the basement. The bulletin invited guests to stop and enjoy something to eat or drink after worship, but there were no directions offered and no signs pointing the way. Those gutsy enough to search the building entered a large gymnasium filled with rows of bare brown rectangular tables, butted end-to-end, running the width of the social hall. A few small groups of regulars seated at the tables stopped talking to watch guests look around the room for an indication of where they might find refreshments. When they finally spotted the open pass-through window between the kitchen and the social hall, they moved along a counter lined with paper bakery bags with undisclosed contents, and clear plastic boxes of store bought cookies with lids ajar and price tags still in tact. At the far end of the counter was a hotplate keeping stale coffee piping hot. Inexpensive and flimsy paper plates, cocktail napkins, and white Styrofoam cups lined the counter next to the coffee. There was a bowl of sugar packets, artificial sweetener, non-dairy creamer and stir sticks. Immediately next to that was a half crushed, unraveling basket that held an uneven piece of brown "shirt" cardboard. Written in letters of varying sizes in black marker was the word "Donations." The word started in the middle of the cardboard and ended with letters crammed together as the writer ran out of space. Standing in the kitchen behind the counter was the group of men and women known as the hospitality committee. They chattered happily until the first time visitors entered the room. Unaccustomed to seeing someone new, they stopped talking and watched with crossed arms as the visitors moved slowly along the counter peeking into sacks in an attempt to identify the contents. One visitor noticed fresh coffee brewing in the large coffee maker at the back of the kitchen. Glancing from the stale coffee on the hot plate to the fresh aromatic brew, he mustered his courage and asked, "Could I have a cup of that fresh coffee?" (Do I really need to finish this story? You already know what happened!) A member of the hospitality committee replied, "No! We have to finish this first!" And another one bit the dust!

This story has a happy ending. That same church came to realize there actually was room in the lobby after all and there were better ways to make a first impression. A small table built to fit in a nook is now covered with linens and decorated with seasonal centerpieces. Pump pots filled with fresh coffee are available, along with all the standard condiments, as well as a variety of plain and flavored creamers.

More attractive cups like those used at the local coffee bar have replaced institutional Styrofoam. (We break out the good china when company is coming, don't we?) The information desk shares its counter space with decorative trays full of homemade iced and decorated cookies. Worshippers gather for refreshments both before and after worship, and the lobby is filled with the sound of fellowship.

In both scenarios, coffee and cookies were offered. The difference is in the focus of the team responsible for refreshments. The first situation describes hospitality of a sort that is focused on the convenience of the team. The second describes high impact hospitality that pays attention to the details and focuses on the needs of the guests. With an outward focus, you serve what appeals to your audience. Goldfish and Mountain Dew might be completely acceptable fare to a young crowd but wouldn't sit well with a congregation over the age of sixty. High impact hospitality means you serve what people like and present it in a highly attractive manner to which the target audience can relate. Whatever is served and however it is presented, high impact hospitality embraces and promotes the culture of excellence to which the church has made a commitment.

SIGNAGE

There are signs everywhere and we live in a culture that depends on signs to get us where we need to go. The same applies to the church. Trying to find a church that is not easily identified can be maddening. High impact hospitality means your facility has an exterior sign that is attractive, unobstructed, and easy to read.

Wandering aimlessly through a building that lacks clear directional signs can cause great anxiety for a visitor. As a young seminary student, Dan had an experience that best exemplifies the hazards of poor signage. He was part of a group of seminarians taken to a church that understood and demonstrated high impact hospitality and they definitely encountered a "WOW" experience. Knowing that most towns in Ohio have two United Methodist churches, and wondering why this particular church was selected over the other, he decided to excuse himself and check out the second church. It didn't take long to locate and he arrived just moments before worship was scheduled to begin. Dan entered through a door he believed to be the main entrance and found no greeter. As a matter of fact, there was no one in sight. He moved through the corridor looking for the entrance to the sanctuary but was unable to find it. His anxiety increased as he turned down hall-way after hallway in search of the correct door. He heard music in the distance and, moving toward it, finally located a door with a small sign above it that said "Sanctuary." Relieved to have finally reached his des-tination, he pulled open the door and stepped directly into the choir loft. Startled choir members stopped singing and turned to stare at a very surprised Dan Glover as the congregation looked on. He quickly jumped back into the hallway, closed the door behind him, and hur-riedly returned to his classmates at the first church. High impact hos-pitality means we help curious visitors overcome their heightened sensitivity by providing attractive interior signs that identify rooms, give directions to common areas such as the nursery, sanctuary, office, etc., and inform people of the day's events, including time and location.

BULLETINS AND ANNOUNCEMENTS

Bulletins are notoriously confusing to visitors because churches tend to communicate in insider language. When the bulletin says, "Heartprints meets tonight at 7:00 p.m. at the home of Todd and Kathy Matthew. Everyone is welcome!" no one will show up except insiders, those already connected to Heartprints or those who personally know where Todd and Kathy live. People new to your church get the message loud and clear. They might be welcome, but they know they aren't really invited. If they were, the bulletin would explain Heartprints and give the Matthew's address and phone number or email address in case visitors have questions or get lost. Bulletin announcements need to be worded in common language and answer in advance questions posed by someone who is either unchurched or new to your congregation.

Regular attendees might have the order of worship memorized, but visitors have no clue what's happening unless it is spelled out in com-mon language and strategically placed in an obvious location in the bulletin. Gather bulletins from other growing, effective churches to help identify a format that will work in your setting. Ask newer atten-dees to your church for constructive feedback that can help you make your bulletin more user-friendly. High impact hospitality means every bulletin:

- Easily guides a visitor through the order of worship;

- Identifies who or what any written announcement concerns and explains the topic of the announcement if it is not self-explana-tory;

- Identifies dates, times, and locations of events and activities;

- Provides a way to get connected: sign up on the spot, stop at a lobby display, contact the person listed (including a phone number and/or email address), just show up, etc.;

- Is written in language easily understood by people who are unchurched or new to your congregation.

At the church where we work, the staff keeps in mind that worship is our widest entry point for visitors, so we do not print anything in the bulletin that targets regular attendees only. What that means for us is we print only announcements that are pertinent to the entire congregation of adults, youth, and children, and have the potential to connect everyone with the discipleship pathway and the life of the church. Team leader share internal communication that applies to small teams or groups such as leadership board meetings, prayer ministry training, band rehearsals, etc. via email, phone call, post card, or letter. Visitors aren't particularly concerned with budget, weekly attendance, or policy decisions, but those same issues are of great interest to regular attendees. Therefore, we communicate that type of information in a monthly newsletter that is mailed to all regular attendees but not to visitors. We use the bulletin as a bridge from worship into the life of the church, and try not to clutter it with information that is irrelevant to a visitor.

We equally target verbal announcements. Announcers conversationally read verbatim carefully worded, strategically selected items that will connect the greatest number of people to the discipleship pathway. We also enhance announcements with electronic images on a large projection screen. High impact hospitality means every verbal announcement:

- Identifies who or what an announcement concerns and explains the topic if it is not self-explanatory;

- Identifies the date, time and location of events and activities or refers people to the bulletin for details;

- Provides a way to get connected: sign up on the spot, stop at a lobby display, contact the person listed (including a phone number and/or email address), just show up, etc.;

- Is explained in language easily understood by people who are unchurched or new to your congregation.

Bulletins and verbal announcements are two of the most important tools you can use to connect the people in your pews to your discipleship pathway. Printing an image of your pathway and brief explanations of core steps in the bulletin will keep your emphasis on discipleship in front of your people every single week. It will also give visitors a view of what your congregation values from the moment they are seated and begin scanning the bulletin. It is a window into the heart of church life. It offers a glimpse of what goes on behind the curtain. How announcements are worded in print and articulated from the stage or chancel speaks volumes to first time visitors.

CHILDCARE

The current generation of young parents, many of whom grew up as latchkey kids, is hesitant to release their children to strangers without assurance they will be safe and secure. Beth visited a church for the first time and left her three-year-old daughter in the nursery while she attended worship. When she returned to pick up her daughter, the child was gone. She angrily asked the childcare servant where her daughter was. The confused servant replied, "I don't know. Maybe she ran out when I wasn't looking." A frantic but brief search located the little girl down the hallway at a water fountain, but the consequences of this lack of security could have been devastating.

High impact hospitality that helps parents overcome their heightened sensitivity means childcare:

- Provides a secure check in and check out procedure;

- Keeps parents connected through an electronic paging system in case the child needs them;

- Is staffed with an appropriate ratio of childcare servants to children;

- Screens childcare servants to insure they are safe people.

There are numerous resources available online, as well as through books, publications, conferences, and seminars that can help you develop a childcare ministry that will be more than your curious visitors expect, create a "WOW" experience, and cause them to feel welcome, expected, and secure.

Once you've assessed and revamped the quality of your hospitality, how do you know if you are being effective? The measure of effective authentic high impact hospitality is the number of first time visitors who return to your church. Once again, it is important to collect accurate attendance information and enter it into a database so you can track not only who is visiting for the first time, but also who is returning.

Follow Up

Following up with first time visitors is vital to the effectiveness of authentic high impact hospitality. Some examples are:

- First time visitor gifts delivered to their home;

- A telephone call from the pastor;

- A phone call from the children's coordinator if visitors brought kids to children's ministry;

- A letter thanking them for visiting.

The more personal the follow up, the greater the impression your church will make. Learn how other growing, effective churches follow up with their first time visitors to help identify a format that will work in your church. Whatever method you choose, a rapid follow up (preferably on same day a guest visits) will have the greatest impact.

Janie is an administrative assistant on the staff of a growing 700-attendance church in the mid-west. For the past year, she repeatedly invited a friend disconnected from church to join her for worship. When the friend finally agreed, she was overwhelmed with what she found. Following the service, she turned to Janie and said, "Wow! This is like church but it's kind of like an event, too!" Later that night, the friend called Janie at home and said, "You'll never guess what happened! Someone brought a bag filled with information about your church and a huge homemade cookie to my home this afternoon. Then, I got a call from your pastor! I couldn't believe it. How did he even know I was there?" Follow up can close the deal. It's that final touch that says, "We've been expecting you and we're very glad you were here."

Janie's friend offered helpful feedback that allowed the staff to know if they were being effective. Offer first time visitors a way to provide anonymous, honest feedback. Ask them what they liked best, what needs improvement, how they learned about the church, how they were treated by your ushers and greeters, etc. It is important that you actually read the responses and make any needed improvements in order to insure you accomplish the objective of authentic, high impact hospitality.

At the end of the day, when first time visitors to your church reflect back on everything they experienced and ask themselves, "What am I going to do about this?" you want them to hold positive memories of being authentically welcomed; of finding more than they ever expected from a church; of encountering a worship experience that was so relevant to their lives that cynicism begins to change to belief that there just might be more to life than they currently know. You want them to find it all so attractive that they will be drawn back to your church for more.

Objective of authentic high impact hospitality: To create an environment that will encourage the curious visitor to return.

Criteria for authentic high impact hospitality: Does this experience overcome the heightened sensitivity of the curious visitor?

Measurement of effectiveness: The number of first time visitors who return.

CHAPTER TEN

Orientation

When I was fourteen, my parents and I traveled to Marblehead, Massachusetts to visit my sister and brother-in-law. As soon as the decision was made to make the trip, Mom called AAA and ordered a TripTik®, one of those neat little packets they put together that includes maps, narrative directions, information on detours, construction zones, and scenic byways, plus tour booklets that identify lodging and restaurants along the way. She read through every piece of the packet before we ever packed our bags and oriented herself to the journey ahead. Dad took a different and less cautious approach to travel. If his destination was located to the north and east of where he was standing, he would jump in the car and alternatively drive north then east until he finally arrived. Travel with Mom was well planned; you knew where you were going and how you were going to get there. Travel with Dad was always an adventure.

Mom was not usually able to sleep in a moving car but, on this particular trip, she became drowsy and simply could not keep her eyes open. We were about 100 miles east of Boston traveling along the Massachusetts Turnpike. Before she nodded off, she instructed Dad to be sure and exit at I-95 so we would travel north and bypass Boston and all its traffic. "Okay" replied Dad, as my mother drifted off to dreamland.

I stared out the window from the back seat and watched the scenery whiz by as we hurried along the busy highway. As the radio played softly and the tires hummed, I noticed a sign for I-95 racing toward us. "Dad, isn't that where we turn?" I asked. "I don't think so" he replied as he blew past the exit. Remember, this was not a man who relied on maps, just instinct.

Mom woke up to the sound of horns blaring in bumper-to-bumper rush hour traffic. She almost jumped out of her skin and cried, "Where are we?" "I think we're in Boston," Dad answered. That's when disorientation set in. None of us knew exactly where we were, we didn't have a clue which road took us toward our destination, and we all had different ideas about how to proceed. We were in unknown territory! It became obvious that we needed to get oriented to our surroundings if we hoped to make any progress, so we put the car in park, brought out the maps, and stayed there until Mom identified a route that would lead us out of our predicament. Before long, we were on our way toward Marblehead once more. Without the maps to guide us, we could have driven aimlessly for hours, simply guessing and trying to figure it out on our own. Isn't that what so often happens in the church?

Disorientation is uncertainty as to direction or confusion about where you are and how to proceed or uncertainty as to direction.[1] The church is unfamiliar territory to curious visitors, and they are disoriented at first. Because the church is so often guilty of providing little to no direction that makes clear the road to spiritual maturity, our congregations slowly fill with people who enter worship, put it in park, and stay there. They need to become oriented to their surroundings and be shown the route that will lead them toward their destination of becoming fully committed followers.

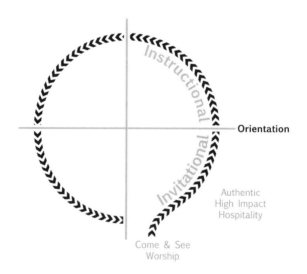

<hr />

[1]Merriam-Webster's Medical Dictionary

When a church neglects to offer clear direction, people begin to guess and try to figure out their own course of action. They connect with a class here and serve there. They try out this event and that opportunity. They reason that a little of this and a little of that just might result in spiritual growth. They eventually group together with other directionless travelers exploring the same path and hope it will lead to their spiritual destination. Before we know it, the church is filled with numerous people groupings, each moving in a different direction.

When authentic high impact hospitality welcomes a person curious enough to actually visit your church, and that person experiences relevant come and see worship, he or she will typically return. Some will continue church shopping and may return later. Those who are not part of the audience you target probably will not come back, but instead move on to another church that is more aligned with their needs. Not every church can or should try to be everything to everybody. Some returning guests will realize after their first few visits that this is exactly what they have been looking for. They've seen the discipleship pathway in the bulletin, had great experiences in the lobby and in worship, and discovered everything they need to know to confidently wade into deeper water. Like Dad, they will jump in the car and take off! There are others, however, who are more like my mother. They require a more complete picture of the church before they actually commit to the journey. They proceed with caution because their sensitivities are still heightened and cynicism is still lurking.

In the crowded lobby between services I heard someone behind me ask, "Can you help me?" I turned to see a woman with an apologetic look on her face. Smiling broadly to help her feel more at ease, I asked, "How can I help you today?" "Well," she said, "I've been coming to church for three months and I want to get involved but I don't know how." Even though we go out of our way to provide clear direction about how to connect to groups, classes, and activities, she obviously needed more information than she had received up to this point. She was still disoriented and needed a bigger picture of the available options, as well as clear, detailed instructions before she could identify and take her next step. "I think Embark would be a great place for you to start." I replied. "Is that the luncheon in the bulletin that you talk about from the stage every week?" she asked. "Yes," I replied. "It's an orientation. We provide a complimentary lunch, Pastor Bill shows a short video about our church, you will meet other people just like you who are new here and have an opportunity to interact with them, hear about the discipleship pathway in a bit more detail, and learn how to take your next step. How does that sound?" I asked. "I don't know. I'm a single mom and I have to get my kids home for lunch right after church. They're starved by then." "That's not a problem," I explained. "We provide lunch for your kids. After lunch there is childcare for little ones in Kindergarten or younger." She raised her eyebrows. "Really? In that case, I'll give Embark a try." Orientation clarifies the process for disoriented people like this single mom.

The objective of orientation is to provide a clear, simple entry point for the curious person who needs to see a bigger picture of the journey ahead before moving forward. Because orientation builds a bridge from stage two to stage three, it is designed to help overcome the primary barrier of stage two (heightened sensitivity) as well as answer the true, underlying question of a person entering stage three (how can I fit in?). That makes orientation a hybrid of invitational discipleship and the next section of the pathway: instructional discipleship.

Making Orientation Effective

An effective orientation overcomes obstacles that might keep people from participating and incorporates high impact hospitality by exceeding the expectations of curious visitors, creating a WOW experience and causing them to feel both welcome and expected.

Extend Repeated Invitations

Effective churches across the country not only print an announcement in the bulletin, but also extend a verbal invitation to orientation every single week. Remember: The goal of the bulletin and verbal announcements is to connect as many people as possible to the discipleship pathway and the life of the church. Your invitation to orientation probably will not register with curious, highly sensitized visitors the first time they hear or read it. Repeated invitations allow them time to settle into their new surroundings, process everything they see and hear, make the decisions about whether they actually want to fit into this particular congregation, and respond at their own pace.

Here is another place where the database we referred to in chapter nine benefits your church. Guests who receive first time visitor follow up require additional follow up as they continue to visit. Their cynicism and sensitivity has probably lessened, but it has not disappeared. Make an additional, non-threatening follow up, such as a letter or postcard from the pastor thanking them for attending worship, inviting them to orientation where they can find out more about the church, meet a few other people, and learn more about the discipleship pathway. This will add to their understanding that you actually value them. If you analyze your attendance data and track visitor trends, you can discover when visitors stop returning if they do not receive additional follow up. At our church, that breakpoint comes after the fourth visit. Therefore, we follow up with a letter of invitation from the senior pastor immediately after the third visit to insure they know we care about their presence in our church.

Make Connection Easy

Whether you register people in advance or ask them to just show up, make it as easy and convenient as possible to get connected to orientation.

If you pre-register, strike while the iron is hot. Provide a way to sign up while they are still seated in worship and the verbal invitation is fresh in their minds. Also, give them the option of contacting the church office to register. Have a host or hostess follow up with a phone call to confirm their registration, thank them for signing up, and answer any questions they might have. This phone call is a great time to find out the names of everyone in the family who will attend and the ages of children. That information is helpful if you plan to prepare nametags or provide childcare.

Even with pre-registration, there will occasionally be someone who asks to attend just minutes before orientation begins. Others will simply drop in. High impact hospitality means you welcome them with open arms and allow them to participate. If you serve a meal, cover your bases by having a few extras on hand for unexpected guests.

Select a Convenient Time and Location

Schedule your orientation at a time and location that is convenient and will make it possible for the greatest number to participate. That's usually immediately following a worship service, when curious visitors are already in your church. Select a room in a convenient location that is easily found by someone unfamiliar with your facility. You may want to post directional signs to help people find their way.

Recruit a Host or Hostess

Assuming the pastor is facilitating orientation and it is offered immediately following worship, it will be difficult for him or her to arrive in time to welcome the first guest. This is an appropriate time to recruit a friendly, outgoing implementer to cover all the administrative details (packets, pens, moving children to childcare, etc.) A host or hostess greeting guests at the door will help put them at ease, especially if that person is the familiar voice who confirmed their registration. "Good morning! You must be Bob and Marsha. Please come in and have a seat. Let me get your nametags for you. The pastor will join us shortly and we'll get started. I'm so glad you've joined us today!" A good host or hostess will direct guests into the room and offer initial instructions. Guests won't feel awkward or have to guess what to do. They will have been given clear direction.

Provide WOW Refreshments

Whether you provide a meal or snacks, serve something unique that is also different from what you serve in the lobby before and after worship. Remember that you are addressing stage two, curious visitors, and authentic *high impact* hospitality will help them overcome their heightened sensitivity.

One church uses the tag line "It's all about the journey!" so they incorporate a hiking theme into their orientation luncheon. Leaders decorate the tables with oversized laminated maps of the Appalachian Trail. The buffet table has a centerpiece that includes a backpack, walking stick, and hiking boots. A hiking boot is the image used in their logo for the class, and a logo sticker decorates the lid of each box lunch. Box lunches include a picnic-style lunch, such as you would take on a day hike: a freshly made six-inch turkey and romaine sub, a dill pickle spear, a small bag of chips and a Journey® Bar.[2] (It's all about the journey! *Journey* Bar? Get it?) Each box also includes a napkin and a condiment packet. They also offer a variety of cold soft drinks, offered in an old tin tub filled with ice and hot coffee. People leave with a great impression and a fully belly.

Because the men and women who attend orientation are stage two visitors in transition to stage three, an effective orientation also incorporates elements of giving and receiving. The objective of giving and

[2]Journey® Bars are made by Keebler, a division of Kellogg Corp.

receiving is to provide wisdom and understanding that leads a believer to explore his or her purpose and call. Granted, they may not be mature enough in their faith at this point to even know they have a God-given purpose, or that God is calling out to them. Nevertheless, the church still bears a responsibility to provide whatever wisdom and understanding they need at this point in their development to lead them toward greater maturity.

Design Format and Content for Strategic Impact

As you design your orientation, all ideas and plans must be filtered through the criteria for establishing an effective offering that truly orients people. Does this experience explain your intentional discipleship plan and clearly identify the next step participants should take? If it does, these curious stage two visitors will garner the information they require to make an informed decision about your church. They will either mentally commit to becoming further involved in the life of your church, or they will move on to another church where their particular spiritual needs can be met.

An effective orientation will provide a view of the church from thirty-thousand feet. This is a "fly by" that gives participants the big picture. It should include:

AN OPPORTUNITY TO BEGIN BUILDING RELATIONSHIPS

In chapter four, *Stage Three: Life in the Waves,* we described two differing philosophies. The first views serving as the road to spiritual maturity. The second views education and relationships that "equip the saints for service" as the pathway to transforming lives. Create an opportunity for stage two travelers who are moving into stage three to begin building relationships with others from the church family. This will set the tone for their entire journey.

Give people a chance to introduce themselves and talk about something personal, such as what they like best about your church, how long they have been attending, where they live, etc. Include time for small group interaction at tables or in groups of four to six.

AN OVERVIEW OF YOUR CHURCH

Give them some history of your church, such as how it started, where the congregation has been, and where it's going. Tell them something about the senior pastor as well so they get an idea of who is leading the way. Cast your vision for the future and explain the mission of the church. For example, the mission of Community Christian Church in Naperville, Illinois is "helping people find their way back to God." The mission of EUM Church in Greenville, Ohio is "preparing people to live for Christ." Articulate your mission, and then briefly explain it.

A short video is a great way to tell the story of your congregation. The lasting impression a quality video can make is worth the cost of hiring a professional if you don't have one on your media team. You can hire one through a local production company, or there may be one available through your denominational headquarters.

SOMETHING FUN TO KEEP IT LIGHT

One church we know has a character named "Sidney Wrongway" drop in to discuss the pitfalls of attempting to reach a destination with no clear direction. The message comes across in a lighthearted way that keeps things upbeat. Another church plays a game that demonstrates the benefits of understanding and following a process. Each person is asked to reach under his or her chair and remove the laminated tag that's attached to the bottom of the seat. Each tag identifies one step in a process. The entire group is given five minutes to get up, compare tags, corporately identify the end result of the process, and then line up in what they believe, with no instruction, is the correct order in which the process takes place. When five minutes is up, the pastor asks the group what they learned from this game about following a process. He or she then reads aloud each step in the correct sequence, and everyone who is out of order relocates to the proper place. The game is loud and rambunctious, and everyone has a great time. They are about to be introduced to the discipleship pathway, and the game is an enjoyable method of educating the group about the value of following an intentional process.

A BRIEF EXPLANATION OF YOUR DISCIPLESHIP PATHWAY

Offer a brief explanation of the overall concept of a discipleship pathway, electives, core classes, and small groups. The entire point of orientation is to help people take their next step on the pathway and move beyond stage two into stage three. Therefore, it is not only unnecessary to explain more than these three steps; it is actually counterproductive to explain beyond the ministries that meet the needs of people at stage three.

A HANDOUT OR INFORMATION PACKET

Provide an attractive handout or information packet participants can follow as you lead them through orientation. Having the same information you present in printed form will allow them to more thoroughly process the information at their own pace once orientation is over.

A handout or packet should include:

- Your vision and mission statements;

- An image of your discipleship pathway;

- Brief descriptions of electives, small groups and each of your core classes.

It might also include:

- Church address, telephone and fax numbers;

- Office hours;

- Website and email address;

- Staff names and extension numbers;

- A map of your facility.

AN EASY WAY TO CONNECT TO THEIR NEXT STEP

Whether it's part of your handout or you hand it to them separately, be sure and have participants complete *and turn in before they leave* a form on which they indicate the next step they plan to take. Provide a way for them to request more information about small groups, electives, and each of your core classes. Also provide a way to offer written comments and request to speak to someone one-on-one about their next step.

This is not the time to ask them to commit to membership, attending a class, or joining a small group. These are curious people who are still testing the water. Giving them the option of receiving more information about areas of interest affords you opportunities to remain in contact with them in a non-threatening way.

You have probably acquired very little information about these people since they are new to the church. Take advantage of your circumstances and gather data that will be invaluable for future reference and follow up. On the next step form, also ask for name; address; home, work and cell phone numbers; email address; occupation; date of birth; name of spouse (if any); and name, gender, and birthdates of their children (if any.) Also ask for feedback. Find out what brought them to orientation so you can assess the effectiveness of your promotion and follow up processes.

Assign someone the responsibility of reading each form and responding to each request for additional information within a day or two following orientation. A personal phone call is most effective. If the host or hostess who originally confirmed their registration and greeted them at orientation also makes the follow up phone calls, their level of comfort will greatly increase. Consistency begets comfort. On the other hand, neglecting to follow up will only heighten sensitivity and increase cynicism, so don't overlook this important step.

Once you've begun offering orientation, how do you know if you are being effective? The measure of effectiveness in orientation is the number of people who identify and take their next step. Record attendance at orientation and enter it into your database. This will allow you to identify who has participated in orientation and if he or she later connects to electives, core classes or small groups. It also allows you to track how many visitors who received letters inviting them to orientation actually attended. If they didn't attend, consider inviting them again.

Orientation creates a platform for the leadership of the church to explain the importance of spiritual development to newcomers. This is your chance to intentionally point the way toward instruction and relationships that can grow people into fully committed followers who serve in response to God's call. Orientation is the map that clarifies the journey ahead as people take their next step and move into stage three.

Objective of orientation: To provide a clear, simple entry point for the curious person who needs to see a bigger picture of the journey ahead before moving forward.

Criteria for authentic high impact hospitality: Does this experience explain your intentional discipleship plan and clearly identify the next step participants should take?

Measurement of effectiveness: The number of people who identify and take their next step.

CHAPTER ELEVEN

Instructional Discipleship

Two roads diverged in the wood and I—I took the one less traveled by,
and that has made all the difference.
The Road Not Taken *by Robert Frost*

When I was in the fifth grade, each student was given the assignment of memorizing a poem and reciting it to the class. I spent hours looking through books of poetry at the local library until I found *The Road Not Taken* by Robert Frost. At the time, I had no idea the significance that poem would hold not only for me personally but also for the church I love and serve.

We have arrived at the fork in the road. This is where so many churches have chosen to follow the road that emphasizes spiritual growth through serving, rather than take the less traveled road that emphasizes discipleship through instruction and relationships. What your church does at this critical juncture will determine the depth to which your parishioners will mature. One way leads to a church filled with actively serving believers, while the other leads to a church filled with spiritually developed servants. As leaders charged with the advancement of God's kingdom, you must know and understand the invisible but very real difference between these two philosophies. As people move into stage three, you must pay close attention to both the conscious and tacit messages conveyed. These messages are the directions that point the way for the people of your church, and how you convey them will make all the difference.

We are not suggesting you forgo recruiting servants until everyone has traveled the entire pathway. There are far too many tasks to be accomplished if the church is to continue functioning. However, if you emphasize service as the primary means of connection, fellowship, and spiritual growth, you encourage people to bypass enormously important steps that are critical to spiritual health and maturity.

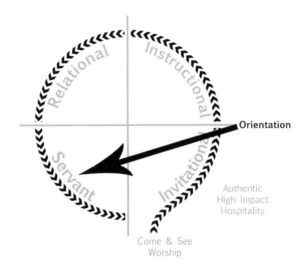

Instructional and relational discipleship is the product of giving and receiving ministries that meet the needs of growing believers as they move through stage three. These ministries lead them into connection and fellowship that can actually result in life transformation. This is where time should be devoted to broadening an understanding of self and the nature of God, as well as the development of trusting relationships. It is where God, through biblical community and careful instruction, can motivate individuals to look inward, identify misconceptions and self-defeating behaviors, and understand the purposes for which they were created. It is in the instructional and relational sections of the pathway that women and men begin to hear the voice of God challenge them to follow into risk-taking service.

In contrast, those who bypass opportunities to become well equipped before venturing into places of influence and leadership in the church typically become casualties that wash ashore, or they create spiritual chaos in the congregation. Therefore, the church must intentionally direct them forward and prepare them for the journey ahead.

Instructional Discipleship

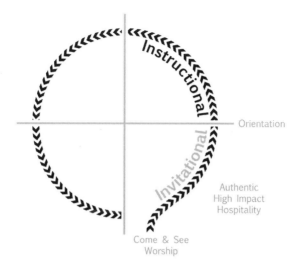

Orientation

Authentic
High Impact
Hospitality

Come & See
Worship

The people in our pews have determined there is benefit derived from the pursuit of a Christian lifestyle or they wouldn't be there. For the most part, they don't know what steps to take beyond worship that will help them grow in their faith. They look to church leadership for direction. Every church has someone preach a weekly sermon, and most churches offer instruction in some form such as Sunday school or midweek classes, but very few develop a comprehensive instructional ministry that systematically equips believers for Christian service. The result has been a hodgepodge of disconnected Bible studies, classes and groups that pass information but do not facilitate transformation.

Our culture understands institutionalized instruction. Children are taken to preschool as early as three years of age to begin receiving instruction that will help them excel and succeed in life. Elementary and secondary education is required in virtually every state in the U.S. Obtaining a post-secondary degree is now commonplace, and many pursue post-graduate degrees even into their senior years. Instruction through the local church, however, has fallen far behind the culture in creating appropriate expectations for learning.

Jesus set clear learning expectations by emphasizing spiritual growth over serving physical needs. In Mark, chapter 2, he entered the home of Simon and Andrew where Simon's mother-in-law lay ill. After healing her, news of the miracle spread to the entire city by sundown. The townspeople made a beeline to Jesus seeking help and he spent the evening curing disease, casting out demons, and meeting a wide array of physical needs. But beginning in verse 35 (NRSV), it becomes evident that, in the context of his ministry, Jesus placed greater emphasis on equipping people for the spiritual journey ahead than on meeting immediate physical need.

"In the morning, while it was still very dark, he (Jesus) got up and went out to a deserted place, and there he prayed. And Simon and his companions hunted for him. When they found him, they said to him, 'Everyone is searching for you.' He answered, 'Let us go onto the neighboring towns so that I may proclaim the message there also; for that is what I came to do.' And he went throughout Galilee, proclaiming the message in their synagogues and casting out demons."

The needs of the people are ever present, and scripture abounds with directives for the church to minister to those needs with compassion and grace. But as we see in this verse, Jesus refocused his ministry back to the purpose for which he was sent: to preach and cast out demons. The objective of the church is no different.

Teaching and preaching (proclamation) are the methods Jesus used to correct misconceptions about God, interpret truth, and equip people with an accurate Christian worldview. Luke 10:38-42 (NIV) paints a clear picture of Jesus directing a believer toward instruction, rather than service as the primary road to spiritual development.

"As Jesus and his disciples were on their way, he came to a village where a woman named Martha opened her home to him. She had a sister called Mary, who sat at the Lord's feet listening to what he said. But Martha was distracted by all the preparation that had to be made. She came to him and asked, 'Lord, don't you care that my sister has left me to do the work by myself? Tell her to help me!' 'Martha, Martha,' the Lord answered, 'you are worried and upset about many things, but only one thing is needed. Mary has chosen what is better, and it will not be taken away from her.'"

Jesus recognized the two differing philosophies—working for Jesus versus being in his presence—and he acknowledged the more beneficial choice.

Jesus identified destructive patterns, challenged people to move beyond them, helped people break free and become all God intended them to be through the casting out of demons. In Mark 5:9 (NRSV), Jesus addresses the demon-possessed man. *"Jesus asked him, 'What is your name?' He replied, 'My name is Legion for we are many.'"* He heals the man before departing for another region, but look how Jesus calls the man into ministry now that his self-defeating behaviors have been addressed. Mark 5:18-20 (NRSV) says,

> "As he (Jesus) was getting in the boat, the man who had been possessed by demons begged him that he might be with him. But Jesus refused, and said to him, 'Go home to your friends and tell them how much the Lord as done for you, and what mercy he has shown you.' And he went away and began to proclaim in the Decapolis how much Jesus had done for him; and everyone was amazed."

This transforming encounter with Jesus better equipped him for service, and he was challenged to return to his hometown and proclaim what God had done for him.

The discipleship pathway to this point has attempted to create comfort for people in stage one and curious stage two visitors. However, when they move past cynicism and heightened sensitivity and demonstrate greater commitment by moving further into the life of the church, they no longer view themselves as visitors but as regular attendees. They have moved into stage three where the necessary comfort they once required now has the potential to become the barrier that can hold them back. And so, like Jesus, the church must create internal spiritual agitation through effective preaching and teaching that stokes the fire burning inside them. Effective preachers, teachers and small group leaders cause us to contemplate and internally wrestle with spiritual issues. They encourage us to move forward and challenge us to be transformed into men and women fully committed to a Christian lifestyle.

Giving and Receiving

Giving and receiving is the primary ministry to people at stage three. The objective of giving and receiving is to provide wisdom and understanding that leads a believer to explore his or her purpose and call. It consists of two components—instruction and relationship. In this instructional discipleship section of the pathway, the focus of giving and receiving is on instruction in classes and support groups that also creates opportunities to build relationships. As you will see in the next chapter, giving and receiving extends into the relational discipleship section of the pathway where the focus is on relationships in small group that also offer instruction. Unless instruction and relationship go hand-in-hand, you will merely pass information. Your people might become well informed but they will not be spiritually transformed into godly men and women who demonstrate the fruit of the spirit and fearlessly follow Jesus. If you want a church filled with world-changers, instruction combined with relationship is key.

Consider the Rhythm of Your Church

Each church has its own rhythm that must be considered when developing this quarter of the pathway. One church may find that people are most available to participate in classes on Sunday morning before, between, or after worship services. Another may find that weeknight classes are better attended. If you currently have a Wednesday night worship service, the addition of classes may be a viable option since your people are already there. Every church is different based on activities that regularly take place at the church, in the school system, and in the local workforce. In other words, scheduling classes and groups in the evening when most of your congregation works second shift at the local factory simply won't work. Scheduling classes on Sunday morning when 65% of your people attend Saturday night worship also will not be effective. If two thirds of your congregation has kids involved in school sports every Monday night, classes probably will not be well attended at that time. Some churches offer classes randomly throughout the year, while others group classes together in six to twelve-week sessions. Researching how other effective churches schedule their instructional opportunities can help you decide what works best in your setting.

Offer Instruction That Also Creates Opportunities to Build Relationships

God wired us for relationship. Just look around and you can see that we were created to interact with others. Consider the explosion in methods of personal communication, including email, online chat rooms, walkie-talkie phones, blogs, text messaging, cell phones, and Blackberries. We crave connection with others and have a deep longing to be known beyond a superficial level of acquaintance or polite friendship.

It is a misconception that the weekly sermon is the primary source of discipleship. It does play a significant role in spiritual development but, standing alone, the sermon will not lead people to the desired destination. Week after week we sit in large group worship services. We may be asked to turn and greet our neighbor, but rarely do we have the opportunity to speak on a deeper level with them. One senior pastor found a congregation of approximately 100 people at the church to which he was newly appointed. Some had attended for fifty years or more, and yet many people on one end of the pew didn't know the names of the people on the other end. This was not an unfriendly church. Everyone greeted each other as they arrived and at the appointed moment in the service, but they never had regular opportunities to build strong, trusting relationships.

When an effective preacher delivers a sermon designed to provoke thought and reflection about a spiritual truth, the church has the opportunity to create arenas in which the resulting spiritual agitation can be addressed, or it can send parishioners on their way in the hope they will figure things out on their own. Left unaddressed, the message tends to dissipate and it slowly fades into the busyness of life. This pattern can repeat week after week, or we can change it by offering classes and groups that are intentionally designed for interaction with other believers—the essence of giving and receiving.

Slight classroom changes can make a huge difference. Rows of folding chairs set up like theater seating are not conducive to intimate conversation. Long narrow tables only allow for conversation with the one or two people seated directly across. Replacing both types of seating with round tables will allow six to eight people to see each other face to face and comfortably interact.

If classes last more than one hour, offer snacks and take a break part way through. People will chat while they grab something to eat or drink.

Open with an icebreaker. For example, ask table groups to tell each other the best thing that happened in the past week, and then give them five minutes to talk together. The question may or may not have anything to do with the lesson, but it will get people talking about something personal but non-threatening. This will help them overcome fears and insecurities while building trust.

The most important thing that can be done to create an opportunity for building relationships is to reject lecture style teaching. Choose curriculum that incorporates opportunities for table group discussion instead. This same opportunity for interaction should be included in any original curriculum that is developed. It is in the midst of discussing the lesson that spiritual agitation begins to be addressed.

People have the opportunity to hear what others are thinking and feeling about the same topics. Thoughts provoked by recent sermons begin to connect to conversations that take place in table groups or over a cup of coffee during the break. People begin to trust that others are genuinely interested in what they have to say, and they are better known than ever before. This is the beginning of healthy biblical community.

Recruit Teachers Who Are Called to Teach

Think back to your school days. Who were the teachers that made the most significant difference? It was those who went the extra mile, wasn't it? They proactively made themselves available to students; they made the lessons fun and exciting; they weren't just putting in time in the classroom; they were passionate about teaching. Those are the people you need leading your classes and groups. Ephesians 3:11 (NIV) says,

> "It was he who gave some to be apostles, some to be prophets, some to be evangelists, and some to be pastors and teachers, to prepare God's people for works of service, so that the body of Christ may be built up until we all reach unity in the faith and in the knowledge of the Son of God and become mature, attaining to the whole measure of the fullness of Christ."

Recruit only those gifted as teachers and passionate about equipping and preparing people to live out their God-given purpose and become mature in their faith. These teachers will go the extra mile and bring props and table decorations as visual aids, use media enhanced curriculum, and throw a "graduation" party at the last session. They will do whatever it takes to make classes and groups exciting. You don't have to settle for less, but you do have to intentionally search for and find them. If you have only one passionate person with the spiritual gift of teaching, use that one to start. Out of one excellent, effective class will come others who have had their internal sparks fanned into flame, and you will then be able to slowly expand your instructional offerings.

Begin with the End in Mind

When we prepare to travel, we look first at the destination, and then identify the route that will take us there. To develop an effective giving and receiving ministry, look first at your destination. In chapter eight, senior pastors were challenged to identify the target by answering the question: "What does a fully committed follower of Jesus Christ look like as a result of being discipled in my church?" The pastor's answer provides a profile toward which the church family must be directed if you intend to reach your desired destination—fully committed followers that look like that profile. If you want your people to become fully committed followers who demonstrate grace and good stewardship, your sermons, classes, and groups must instruct your people in those areas. If you want them to demonstrate servanthood, unity in the body, and the priesthood of all believers, then these areas must be the focus of your instruction. Your congregation will grow into the expectations you set before it.

Point Your People in the Right Direction

Pointing parishioners in the right direction is not difficult if every choice offered is a correct choice. Classes and groups designed to instruct people in the "how to" of Christian living must be focused on three primary topics: theology, spiritual disciplines and practical application of scriptural truth. If every class or group falls into one of these three categories, it's impossible to fail in making a beneficial selection. They will all be beneficial in moving people toward the destination of becoming fully committed followers.

If you have any college experience, you are familiar with the concept of core classes. The faculty identifies specific information it expects every student to possess by the time students receive their diplomas. In other words, they have created a profile of what a graduate looks like as a result of being educated in their university. That core information is taught in classes every student is required to complete prior to graduation.

College also offers electives that vary from student to student depending on what is needed to obtain a degree in their chosen course of study. The needs of a student majoring in horticulture will differ from the needs of a student majoring in electrical engineering. The interests of a student with artistic abilities may differ from the interests of a student with athletic abilities, and those differences will be reflected in the electives they choose.

The instructional section of an effective discipleship pathway incorporates the concept of core and elective offerings. Core classes teach what every Christian must know, while electives cover topics that meet the varied needs and interests of many people. As you develop giving and receiving ministries, all of your ideas and plans must be filtered through the criteria for effectiveness in this area. Do the collective instructional discipleship opportunities equip a person to better understand his or her purpose and call? It will require thoughtfulness and careful planning with a clear focus on the destination. With that in mind, you can begin developing core classes and electives that have the potential to move your congregation toward real life change.

As a word of caution, don't expect everyone to take classes in the order in which they are arranged within the instructional section of the pathway. Some will choose to move sequentially from one step to the next, while others will bypass electives and go right to core beliefs. Still others will bypass electives and core beliefs and move directly to core principles. Many will repeatedly choose elective and continue to participate in them year after year. It is most effective to allow people to move a their own pace, while continually encouraging them to move forward.

Develop Electives

An effective discipleship pathway will include a variety of relevant elective classes and groups that provide attractive entry points to people in stage three. Electives should target three foundational areas of study, and each class and group you consider must be filtered through the criteria for choosing effective options. Do these classes effectively teach theology, spiritual disciplines and the practical application of scripture?

Theology is the study of God and God's relation to the world. A theology-based class may study a book of the Bible, offer a topical study, provide an overview of the Old or New Testament, or take a class through the entire Bible. Theology-based classes develop greater understanding of the character and nature of God and correct previously held misconceptions about God. Growing believers must learn to appropriately relate to God in order to step out in faith and follow God as they move forward on their journey.

According to Richard Foster in his classic book, *Celebration of Discipline* (HarperCollins: New York, 1978), spiritual disciplines are " . . . a means of receiving God's grace. (They) allow us to place ourselves before God so he can transform us." Foster says that spiritual disciplines are like a narrow ridge with a sheer drop-off on either side.

There is the abyss of trust in works on one side, and the abyss of faith without works on the other. On the ridge there is a path that represents the disciplines of the spiritual life. He says we must always remember that the path does not produce change; it only places us where change can occur. A class devoted to spiritual disciplines may provide an overview of a variety of disciplines, or an in-depth study of one particular discipline such as solitude, silence, fasting, sacrifice, study, prayer, tithing, etc. Growing believers learn to hear and recognize God's voice through the practice of spiritual disciplines.

Classes that teach how to apply scriptural principles in relevant, practical situations develop life skills in a growing believer that are consistent with a Christian worldview. It may be a class that teaches debt reduction or personal money management, parenting skills, marriage enrichment, establishing personal boundaries, discerning safe from unsafe people, surviving marriage to an unbeliever, etc. Christian life skills may also be taught through support groups that deal with grief, addictions, divorce recovery, or physical conditions such as diabetes, cancer, MS, etc. Practical application electives are the means by which new and rededicated believers learn how to make different choices in their day-to-day lives that can move them toward living a committed Christian lifestyle.

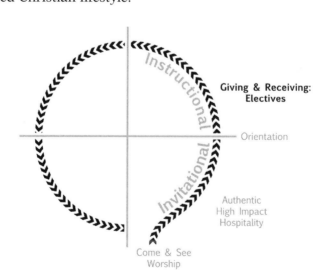

Once you've begun offering elective classes and groups that meet criteria, how do you know if you are being effective? The measure of effectiveness in elective offerings is qualitative—new understandings are reflected in personal choices.

Janie is a great example. She was still in her twenties when we met, in her third marriage with three children by two different husbands. In spite of growing up in a highly dysfunctional home, Janie had developed a strong work ethic and sense of responsibility that allowed her to be the primary breadwinner for her family.

Janie had a desperate quality about her. She would grab me whenever we met and give me a huge bear hug. "I love you," she would tell me, even though we barely knew each other. She always had a look in her eyes, as though she wanted to tell me something more but couldn't quite bring herself to say it. "Pray for me," she would shout over her shoulder as she walked away. As time passed, she slowly began revealing bits of information that indicated her marriage was experiencing fairly significant problems. She eventually sought advise from both Dan and me in her search for a way to fix her marriage. Being married three times was humiliating enough, and another divorce seemed too much to endure. She was willing to try almost anything.

One particular Wednesday night just twenty minutes before a new twelve-week session of adult classes began, Janie showed up with eyes swollen from crying. I cornered her and asked for the whole truth. She was at the end of her rope, and finally confessed that her husband was physically abusing her as well as one of her daughters. Janie was a textbook co-dependent and didn't even know it. She told me she had signed up for a parenting class because she thought it might save her marriage if she could just become a better mother. I urged her to reconsider and attend *Boundaries*[1] instead. She reluctantly agreed, but only if I would accompany her to the parenting class and explain to the teacher why she was making a switch. "Not a problem," I said. "Let's go."

Janie's first night in *Boundaries* was highly emotional. She was shocked by the insights she immediately gained into her own self-defeating behavior patterns, and surprised by the continued internal agitation she experienced throughout the week that followed. She stopped me between services the following Sunday and told me about her experience with the class. And thus began Janie's transformation.

The wisdom and understanding Janie gained not only from *Boundaries*, but also from an array of electives and core classes she took over the next two and a half years, equipped her to make healthier choices that are consistent with a committed Christian lifestyle. Janie put herself and her children in professional counseling and went

[1]*Boundaries,* Drs. Henry Cloud and John Townsend (Zondervan: Grand Rapids, MI, 1992).

through a difficult divorce. In spite of that, her level of self-esteem skyrocketed. In the past she was a woman whose home and personal appearance mirrored the emotional chaos inside. But Janie has transformed into a woman who cares for herself physically, emotionally, and spiritually. You will know your elective classes are effective when students make personal choices that reflect new understandings they have been taught.

> **Criteria for electives:** Do these classes effectively teach theology, spiritual disciplines and the practical application of scripture?
> **Measurement of effectiveness:** New understandings are reflected in personal choices.

Develop Core Classes

An effective discipleship pathway will include two core classes. One will teach the core beliefs of the Christian faith. The other will teach the core principles established by the senior pastor when he answered the question, "What does a fully committed follower of Jesus Christ look like as a result of being discipled in my church?"

Core Beliefs

My husband, Keith, grew up in a Christian home. His parents took him to church every Sunday, and they were intentional about demonstrating their faith through lifestyle choices. Everyone in his world tried to live a life pleasing to God, but no one specifically instructed him in the basic beliefs of the Christian faith. He assumed he was a Christian because Christians raised him. In other words, he thought he became a Christian by osmosis.

Keith stopped attending church when he left home at age eighteen. As an adult, he was a good person who tried to follow the Golden Rule and the Ten Commandments, and he didn't see any reason to continue to attend. In his mind the church had accomplished its goal while he was growing up by producing a really nice man. But all that changed when personal crisis struck at age forty, and he suddenly realized he was lost. A friend invited him to lunch, gave him a Bible, and led him into a personal relationship with Christ over hamburgers and french fries. Keith returned to church as a new believer, but soon realize he didn't understand the basics of the faith as he listened to the sermon each week.

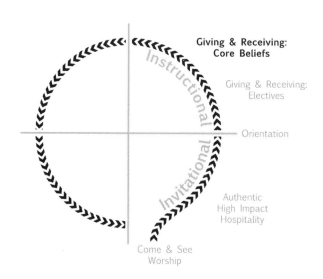

The church is woefully guilty of assuming everyone who sits in the pews is familiar with the core beliefs of Christianity. That's simply not true. To insure new and rededicated believers at stage three have a strong spiritual foundation upon which to build, the church must offer a class that focuses on core beliefs. We're not talking about denominational basics, because the church was never commissioned to go and make Methodists or Baptists or Pentecostals of all nations. We're talking about the foundational beliefs of the Christian faith that cross denominational lines—God, Jesus, the Holy Spirit, salvation, the Bible, prayer, etc. These are the non-negotiable foundational beliefs upon which the faith of every Christian stands and by which the Christian faith is characterized. How to baptize, when to baptize, what to wear, whether to dance or watch movies are not core beliefs, but are interpretation of scripture that vary from denomination to denomination.

The curriculum for your core beliefs class might be purchased, original curriculum you write, or a combination of the two. You may find existing curriculum that covers core beliefs in exactly the way you believe they should be taught. However, if what you find is close yet not quite what you where hoping for, you can use it until you find something better, or you create your own. You might combine original material with the use of an existing book or study guide. Whether you purchase or create your own, the material you use must align with the core beliefs of the senior pastor so the message conveyed from the pulpit is consistent with instruction presented in the classroom.

Some of you are thinking, "Are they kidding? We can't write original curriculum! We don't know how!" Don't fool yourself. You are far more capable than you realize. Here's the reality of writing original curriculum for the church: Senior pastors know exactly what beliefs they consider core, and are able to articulate their thoughts on each. Those thoughts can be put in writing, even if it's bad writing. Someone on your staff or in your congregation has the ability to write well and edit those thoughts into clearly articulated material. Someone on your staff or in your congregation is able to discern good curriculum from bad, and is able to format what has been written into a usable end product. As your core beliefs teacher presents this original curriculum, it won't take long to find out what works and what doesn't. Evaluate the material after every class and rework the parts that are not effective. Throughout the process, it is the responsibility of senior pastor to insure the doctrinal integrity of the material being written. Before you know it, you will have carved out a curriculum that both pleases you and conforms to the criteria for an effective core beliefs class, affirmatively answering the question, "Does this class effectively teach the basic beliefs every Christian must understand?"

A core beliefs class is not deep theology. It is Christianity 101 and should be easily grasped by previously unchurched, new believers. Actually, there will be people in your core beliefs class who have not yet accepted Christ because they may not know anything about salvation (a core belief). First Corinthians 2:14-16 (NIV) says:

> "The man without the Spirit does not accept the things that come from the Spirit of God, for they are foolishness to him, and he cannot understand them, because they are spiritually discerned. The spiritual man makes judgments about all things, but he himself is not subject to any man's judgment: 'For who had known the mind of the Lord that he may instruct him?' But we have the mind of Christ."

What that means is the people in your classroom who have not yet accepted Christ will not be transformed because they simply cannot hear or understand a thing you are saying. Their spirits are not yet alive in Christ. Therefore, the first session of an effective core beliefs class should offer an explanation of salvation by grace through faith in Jesus Christ, and include an invitation to accept a personal relationship with him.

These same unsaved people who do not yet understand things that come from the Spirit of God may have participated in electives as well, but that does not mean the teaching they received will go to waste. Those electives may not have provided a transformational experience for them at that time, but the Holy Spirit who "guides you into all truth" (John 16:13 NIV), and continues to teach long after class has ended, will bring those lessons to mind at the right time to serve God's purposes.

Once you've begun offering your core beliefs class, how do you know if you are being effective? The measure of an effective core beliefs class is qualitative: Christian beliefs and a hunger to understand more about God and self are articulated outside of class. The conversation and language of those who complete a core beliefs class begins to reflect qualities instilled by the instruction. They begin to articulate new wisdom and understanding. You will hear students say something like, "I had no idea that's how a person becomes a Christian! I thought you just had to be a good person." Or, "I tried reading the Bible once and it didn't make any sense. Now I understand how it applies to me and I can't wait to learn more."

Because those who take your core beliefs class may not have attended orientation, once again take advantage of your captive audience and gather information that will be invaluable for future reference and follow up. Provide a registration form at the first session that asks for name; address; home, work and cell phone numbers; email address; date of birth; occupation; name of their spouse (if any); and name, gender and birthdates of their children (if any.) This data, as well as class attendance, should be entered into your database. Ask for feedback, such as what brought them to your church or to the core beliefs class. This will help you evaluate your methods of connecting people to your church and your discipleship pathway.

To encourage participants to move forward on the discipleship pathway, be sure and have participants complete and turn in at the last class session a form on which they indicate the next step they plan to take. You can expect a greater level of commitment from people at stage three than you could from the curious stage two visitors who attended orientation, so provide a way for them to sign up for the next session of your core principles class, connect to a small group, get more information about electives, and personally speak to someone about their next step. Remember to have someone actually read these forms and quickly follow up.

Core Principles

The senior pastor establishes core principles when he or she answers the question, "What does a fully committed follower of Jesus Christ look like as a result of being discipled in my church?" People need an arena where they come face to face with Christ's expectations for his followers and personally wrestle through the relevance of those principles to their daily lives. Your pastor can effectively deliver a yearly series of twenty-minute sermons devoted to your core principles, and you can list them in your newsletter and paint them on the wall of your lobby. But until growing believers experience a giving and receiving opportunity where they can discover how those principles personally apply to them, they will not have an opportunity to experience real life change.

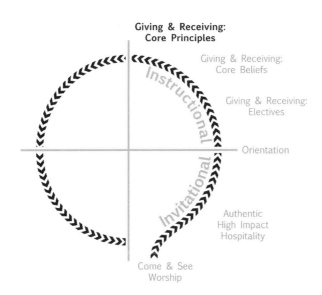

Once stage three believers have moved through orientation, experienced elective classes and groups, and participated in a core beliefs

class, they will have matured in their faith to the point where they are prepared to make a greater commitment to the church. An effective core principles class introduces believers to the realities of living a committed Christian lifestyle.

There may be people in your core principles class with prior church experience and enough basic knowledge to bypass the core beliefs class who have not yet accepted Christ. To insure you are teaching those who are spiritually equipped to understand spiritual things, the first session of an effective core principles class should explain salvation by grace through faith in Jesus Christ, and include an invitation to accept a personal relationship with him.

To be effective, the curriculum for your core principles class must be customized to the core principles established by the senior pastor. You may find several existing curricula from which you can combine excerpts until your entire core principles are covered, but a truly effective class will offer original curriculum that transmits the "DNA" of your church to each class participant. The material you develop must conform to the criteria for an effective core principles class: "Does this class effectively teach the non-negotiable values of a fully committed follower?"

A core principles class provides a perfect platform for discussing church membership, particularly if one of your core principles pertains to biblical community, covenant relationships or the integrity of commitment to the body of Christ. Because you are addressing believers who have developed a higher level of commitment to the church, this is the best opportunity to share denominational doctrines and membership expectations or requirements. The core principles class in our church is six weekly, two-hour sessions, and is a pre-requisite for membership. The option to join the membership of the church is presented at the last session, and people may choose at that time. Baptism for those who accepted Christ during the six weeks of class is scheduled for the Sunday following the last class. Induction into membership is scheduled for the Sunday after baptism. But only a small portion of class time is devoted to membership in the local church. Therefore, we do not promote it as a membership class. We promote it as an introduction to a committed Christian lifestyle, and point out that this class is a prerequisite to membership. The emphasis is placed on commitment. As a result, those who join are highly committed to a common set of core beliefs and core principles.

Once you've begun offering your core principles class, how do you know if you are being effective? The measure of an effective core principles class is qualitative: Disparity and a hunger to understand more about God and self are articulated outside class. The conversation and language of those who complete a core principles class reflect qualities instilled by the instruction. They begin to see the disparity between their cultural view of life and a Christian worldview, and they will articulate their new wisdom and understanding. "I thought I was doing the right thing but now that I've learned more about servanthood, I realize I've been motivated more by my own agenda than by the love and mission of Christ." "This class has really changed my perspective on stewardship and I need to learn more. When does that money management class start?"

Because those who take your core principles class may not have attended orientation or the core beliefs class, once again take advantage of your captive audience and ask for the same information you requested on your core beliefs registration form. This data, along with class attendance, should be entered into your database.

This time, instead of asking for feedback, consider asking them to briefly share something about themselves that would help you know them better. Notice that the requests for comments and feedback become progressively more personal as people move from orientation, to core beliefs, to core principles. Moving people toward intimate conversation by seating them in table groups, providing adequate time for personal interaction with other growing believers, and asking progressively more personal but appropriate questions will help prepare them for their next step into a small group.

To encourage participants to move forward on the discipleship pathway, be sure and have participants complete and turn in at the last class session a form on which they indicate the next step they plan to take. Believers at this stage have worked their way along half of the pathway, so you can expect them to demonstrate an increased level of commitment. Provide a way for them to not only get connected to a small group, but also find out more about leading a small group. Entire groups that first met in your core beliefs class will often move together into your core principles class, especially if you offer the two classes back-to-back. These people who shared thoughtful, intimate discussions about their beliefs and lifestyles in a table group often decide to form a small group once the classes are over. Remember to have someone actually read these forms and quickly follow up.

> **Criteria for core principles:** Does this class effectively teach the non-negotiable values that drive a fully committed follower?
>
> **Measurement of effectiveness:** Disparity and a hunger to understand more about God and self are articulated out of class.

Assess the Effectiveness of Instructional Discipleship

Once you have begun moving people through the giving and receiving opportunities that constitute the instructional section of your discipleship pathway, how do you know if you are being effective? The number of people who begin exploring their purpose and call will determine the effectiveness of giving and receiving opportunities. People will begin approaching the senior leadership of the church and ask, "Can I meet with you? I think God's trying to tell me something and I need help figuring this out." Or they may send a letter of testimony to the pastor telling of the positive changes that are taking place in their life as a result of their experiences in classes and groups. In whatever form these indicators appear, the people of your church will begin letting you know that God is moving them forward, and they are eager to understand more about the purpose for which they were created.

At this point in the journey, you may also hear people ask, "Aren't there any classes with more meat?" The natural tendency is to think we need deeper Bible study when, in reality, we need deeper relationship.

I once formed a small group for the specific purpose of developing men and women with strong leadership abilities into intentional disciple makers. At our second meeting, I asked everyone what he or she expected of this group. When I got to Mike he said, "I don't mean to sound arrogant, but I've seen it all and heard it all and there's got to be more to the Christian life then where I am today." Mike was a lifelong Christian. He had listened to sermons since he was a child, and taken every class offered at the various churches he attended. While he possessed a broad intellectual knowledge of the Bible and was sure of his salvation, he had not experienced the abundant life described in scripture. He had not experienced transformation and, just as we described in stage four of the ocean diagram, Mike's question was, "Is there anything else?" He needed a different type of giving and receiving, and the relationships he was about to build in small group would make all the difference.

Objective of giving and receiving: To provide wisdom and understanding that leads a believer to explore his or her purpose and call.

Criteria for giving and receiving: Do the collective discipleship opportunities equip a person to better understand his or her purpose and call?

Measurement of effectiveness: The number of people who begin exploring their purpose and call.

CHAPTER TWELVE

Relational Discipleship

When Mike said, "I've seen it all and heard it all and there's got to be more to the Christian life then where I am today", he identified himself as a man on the same quest as the rich young man in Mark 10:17-19 (NIV). The young man asks Jesus, *"What must I do to inherit eternal life?"* Jesus answers, *"Do not murder, do not commit adultery, do not steal, do not give false testimony, do not defraud, honor your father and mother."* The young man replies, "But Jesus, I've seen it all, I've heard it all and I'm doing all these things. There's got to be more to the Christian life than where I am today!" That's when Jesus told the young man it was time to take all the knowledge he had acquired from all his years of instruction and actually incorporate it into his lifestyle in such a way that it would allow him to live like Jesus. The disappointed young man basically said, "I don't think so!" and turned away. Giving up everything meant he would have nothing on which to depend; he would no longer be self-sufficient; he would become vulnerable. His ability to succeed would no longer depend on the possessions he owned, but instead on his ability to develop healthy inter-dependent relationships.

According to the Merriam Webster dictionary, a disciple is one who accepts and assists in spreading the doctrines of another, a convinced adherent of an individual or school of thought. Therefore, discipleship is the act of spreading the doctrines of another by convinced adherents of Jesus Christ. Luke 9:23 (NIV) says, *"If anyone would come after me, let him deny himself and take up his cross daily and follow me."* This is the essence of discipleship—spreading the doctrines of Jesus in ways that can transform others into convinced adherents of him. Becoming a disciple, however, takes more than simply acquiring knowledge, because knowing you must take up his cross daily is entirely different than actually taking up his cross and following him. For the rich young man, moving beyond his comfort zone was simply too high a price to pay to live like Jesus. In contrast, Mike chose to move forward and explore the world of healthy inter-dependent relationships, in spite of the inherent risks that come with being vulnerable.

Relational Discipleship

The church most often equates discipleship with one-on-one relationships similar to Mr. Myiagi teaching Daniel LaRusso the secrets of the masters in *The Karate Kid*. However, as we look back over the first half of the pathway, we can see that discipleship is much more comprehensive. There are many intangible aspects of discipleship that spread the doctrines of Christ to people at various stages of spiritual development, including:

- Come and see worship to which unchurched people intangibly relate;

- Authenticity and hospitality that create intangible comfort for curious believers;

- Orientation that intangibly points the way toward further spiritual growth;

- Classes and groups that instruct new and rededicated believers in the intangible knowledge of the Christian faith.

No wonder those areas are typically overlooked! One must peer deeply into the invisible world of the spirit to actually "see" them. As a result of overlooking those critical initial steps of faith formation, many churches attempt to place people who are unequipped for deeper relationships in small groups. The hope is that lives will be transformed but, instead, they very often end up with a bunch of Bible studies that rehash the same old lessons or groups that devolve into superficial fellowship. However, when a church intentionally leads people through invitational and instructional discipleship first, relational discipleship can become powerful and life changing.

Right from the start, God created us to be in relationship. Genesis 1:27-28a (NRSV) says, "*So God created man in his own image, in the image of God he created them; male and female he created them. God blessed them and said to them . . .*" God immediately talked with us and gave us the ability to talk with God. God then gave humankind purpose. *"Be fruitful and increase in number; fill the earth and subdue it. Rule over the fish of the sea and the birds of the air and over every living creature that moves on the ground"* (Genesis 1:28b NRSV). Once God established relationship with us and identified our purpose, God established the beginning of biblical community. *"The Lord God said, 'It is not good for the man to be alone. I will make a helper suitable for him'"* (Genesis 2:18 NRSV). God's original intent is for men and women to communicate with God and with each other as they live out the purposes for which God created them. Obviously, Adam and Eve messed all that up, but Christ has given us the opportunity to be restored to the original intent of creation, to reestablish our relationship with God and one another. Invitational discipleship invites us to receive this opportunity for restoration. Instructional discipleship teaches about the many aspects of restoration. Relational discipleship is the mechanism through which we actually participate in the restoration of others and ourselves to an understanding and practice of God's original intent for us, God's beloved creation.

By and large, this view of relational discipleship has not been practiced in the church. Instead, we have acquiesced to the concept of friendship. Don't we all seek a "friendly" church? "We tried First Church last Sunday and they were very 'friendly!' I think we'll go back." Of course, the very essence of invitational discipleship is creating an environment where people feel welcome and invited. However, the church has taken discipleship even beyond the invitational stage and replaced it with less potent friendliness. Granted, friendship is not a bad thing in and of itself, but the church is not commissioned to make friends. It is commissioned to make disciples. We begin to see the reason for the lack of life transformation in the church when we compare the definitions of disciple and friend:

- **Disciple**—One who accepts and assists in spreading the doctrines of another as one of the twelve in the inner circle of Christ's followers according to the Gospel accounts; a convinced adherent of a school or individual.

This is a description of the men and women God expects the church to produce.

- **Friend**—One attached to another by affection or esteem; acquaintance.

- **Acquaintance**—A person with whom one is acquainted; a person whom one knows but who is not a particularly close friend.

This is a description of the women and men the church is currently producing because it has taken its eyes off the destination. Friends have no motivation to spread the doctrines of Christ because there is no expectation placed upon them to do so by their church-based relationships.

Disciples accept the doctrines of Jesus and make them their own. Jesus' doctrines become the core principles that drive disciples as they emulate Jesus' lifestyle. Like the Twelve, they are equipped to spread these doctrines beyond themselves into the lives of others. Accepting the doctrines of Jesus is not a pre-requisite for friendship. Because friends are attached by tender feelings (affection), high regard (esteem), or simply because they are acquainted rather than by passionate, shared conviction, there is no compelling drive to emulate Jesus' lifestyle. Is it any wonder the church has lost its ability to influence the culture? Jesus was a radical, passionate, spiritual "terrorist" who systematically used the power of God to spread his doctrines and transform others into adherents. In John 15:15 (NRSV), Jesus told his disciples, *"No longer do I call you servants, for the servant does not know what his master is doing; but I have called you friends, for all that I have heard from my Father I have made known to you."* Notice that Jesus *first* called them servants, meaning they took instruction and direction from him while they were being discipled. After they had reached a more significant level of spiritual maturity, he then called them friends. Proverbs 12:26a (NIV) warns, *"A righteous man is cautious in friendship . . ."* The church should heed these words and recognize that friendship is not the purpose of biblical community. The purpose is relational discipleship and out of this will grow deep, intimate friendships.

When discipleship is reduced to another Bible study or a small group of people who get together for dinner and Pictionary©, the church becomes filled with friendly people who may be able to quote chapter and verse but lack the love, joy, peace, patience, kindness, goodness, faithfulness, gentleness, and self-control that are the demonstrable qualities that separate the sheep from the goats.

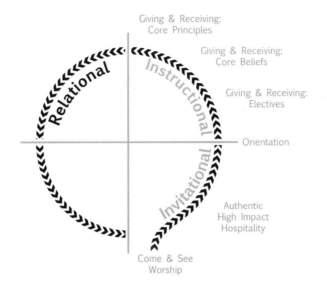

Giving & Receiving:
Core Principles

Giving & Receiving:
Core Beliefs

Giving & Receiving:
Electives

Relational

Instructional

Invitational

Orientation

Authentic
High Impact
Hospitality

Come & See
Worship

Relational discipleship proactively equips people for the journey ahead. It does not wait for a person to crash and burn before helping repair the damage but, instead, enters into a more intimate relationship that equips people for life in the deep. Relational discipleship does not say, "Go ahead and swim out into deep water. When the sharks tear you up, drag yourself back here and we'll tell you what you should have done differently." Effective relational discipleship says, "Let's develop enough trust to seek biblical direction and guidance from one another and avoid the sharks." Therein lies the rub. Intimate, trusting relationships seem so personal, intrusive, and uncomfortable. Therefore, we tend to pull our punch to maintain an acceptable level of emotional comfort. We fall into the trap of "good Christian" behavior and never talk with each other about dreams, fears, desires, or the unresolved issues that haunt us—the real stuff that drives us forward in what we hope is the right direction. We are left to figure it out on our own outside of biblical community (God's original relational intent for us) and we often find ourselves in over our heads, surrounded by sharks just waiting to tear us apart.

Relational discipleship is devoted to building healthy biblical community where people can appropriately work through new information they gain from preachers and teachers. They learn to incorporate it into everyday life, correctly interpret God's voice, and wrestle through the roller coaster ride of discerning their God-given purpose. It is in the giving and receiving of encouragement, confession, direction and guidance, accountability, and loving confrontation that the Holy Spirit begins to transform us into the likeness of Christ. Ephesians 4:11-16 (NIV) says:

> "It was he who gave some to be apostles, some to be prophets, some to be evangelists, and some to be pastors and teachers, to prepare God's people for works of service, so that the body of Christ may be built up until we all reach unity in the faith and in the knowledge of the Son of God and become mature, attaining to the whole measure of the fullness of Christ. Then we will no longer be infants, tossed back and forth by the waves, and blown here and there by every wind of teaching and by the cunning and craftiness of men in their deceitful scheming. Instead, speaking the truth in love, we will in all things grow up into him who is the Head, that is, Christ. From him the whole body, joined and held together by every supporting ligament, grows and builds itself up in love, as each part does its work."

In other words:

- God has gifted each of us for the purpose of equipping others to serve God;

- The purpose of equipping people is to bring the church to an understanding of Jesus that results in Christ-like maturity and unity;

- When people reach that level of maturity, they will no longer react inappropriately to everything that is said and done inside or outside the church;

- Instead, they will lovingly confront one another because that is the process that leads to spiritual maturity;

- When the whole congregation recognizes this process as the face of biblical love and willingly submits to it, each person will serve according to God's purpose and call.

What we call direction, guidance, and encouragement, the apostle Paul calls "growing and building up." What we call confession, accountability and loving confrontation, Paul calls "speaking the truth in love." The use of these tools is the foundation of an effective giving and receiving ministry.

Moving People from Stage Three to Stage Four

Authentic high impact hospitality creates comfort. Effective instructional giving and receiving introduces new perspectives that create disparity between cultural and biblical lifestyles. Disparity brings with it a dawning realization that things are not as they should be and an increasing sense of discomfort. While comfort was once vital to spiritual development, it now can become the very barrier that stops stage three believers from moving forward. They look for ways to release the pressure caused by the internal spiritual agitation. There are only three ways to find relief: (1) repress the agitation, justifying a cultural lifestyle and conform to the status quo; (2) attempt to separate from the agitation by leaving the church (this often leads to church hopping in search of refuge from the agitation); or (3) take intentional steps to move outside the comfort zone, beyond the agitation and continue pursuing God's plan for their lives. If people choose to move forward into deeper water, they soon feel their feet come off the bottom with a little voice inside crying, "Go back to the beach! The water is over your head! You're gonna drown!" And yet it is only by stepping out in faith that a person can continue to pursue God's purpose and call. As John Ortberg puts it, "If you want to walk on water, you've got to get out of the boat."

Small Groups and Spiritual Growth

The objective of small groups is to provide an emotionally safe environment where a believer's spiritual agitation can be appropriately addressed. Small groups are designed to focus primarily on deeper relationships, not instruction, service, or fellowship. Each is an important aspect of discipleship, but the function of an effective small group is to overcome the primary barrier to further spiritual development faced by stage three believers—comfort. That being the case, the role of the small group leader is to create a trust-filled environment where people can safely confess their God-dreams, their spiritual agitation can be addressed, and the group can fan each person's internal flame into a raging inferno. Those internal fires motivate the group to move forward.

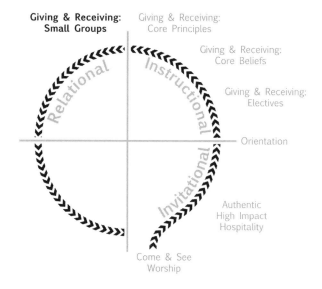

Giving & Receiving:
Small Groups

Giving & Receiving:
Core Principles

Giving & Receiving:
Core Beliefs

Giving & Receiving:
Electives

Orientation

Authentic
High Impact
Hospitality

Come & See
Worship

Relational

Instructional

Invitational

When Mike joined my small group, his wife Teri joined as well. They were a rather private couple that typically spent time together or with family. As we mentioned in chapter eleven, Mike was a lifelong Christian. He grew up in a Christian home and graduated from twelve years of Christian schooling. He was a quiet intellectual, with an extensive amount of biblical knowledge. While Mike regularly pondered scripture, he was not particularly self-aware and found personal disclosure difficult. It's not that he was unwilling to share, he just couldn't think of anything to say. He was taught to look outward and serve others. Looking inward seemed almost selfish to him.

Teri grew up in a highly dysfunctional home with an absent father and an alcoholic mother. She had a son out of wedlock and lived in an unmarried relationship with the child's drug addicted father, but eventually moved out and raised her son alone. Teri became a Christian as an adult. When we first met, she had unresolved issues that kept her stuck in self-defeating behavior. Teri had a sarcastic edge and held a generally pessimistic view of life.

On week one of our small group, we each shared our individual faith stories. We explained how we got from birth to the church we currently attended and identified significant spiritual landmarks along the way that helped shape our view of the world. On week two, I asked each person what he or she expected from this small group experience. Mike's response was a paraphrase of the primary question "Is there anything else?" that identified him as a person at stage four. Teri crossed her arms, scrunched down in the couch and frowned. "I have no idea!" she snapped.

As Teri slowly learned to trust others in the group, she opened up and confessed her great anger with God for allowing her to suffer through childhood in a terribly unhappy and destructive home. The group realized she was stuck in her unresolved issues and challenged her to get connected to a solid Bible study that would help her have a more accurate view of God. We offered guidance to connect with a support group that addressed co-dependency issues and direction regarding how to maneuver through difficulties she experienced in ministry that were a result of her emotional wounds that had not healed. When Teri allowed herself to slip into the role of a victim, the group lovingly confronted her and held her accountable for moving forward. Over the course of eighteen months, Teri followed every direction she was given (even though she sometimes didn't want to), stepped out of her comfort zone, and began to transform from unhappy and suffering to an upbeat, vibrant young woman. She enrolled in college and began pursuing a degree she had longed for.

Over time, Mike witnessed a 180-degree turnaround in Teri and tearfully prayed at the end of one small group meeting, "Thank you, Father, for giving me back my wife." He recognized that transformation by the "renewing of your mind" is accomplished through deeper relationship, not deeper Bible study. Like Teri, Mike moved outside his comfort zone and developed more intimate relationships than he had ever experienced. He was also afforded opportunities to facilitate leadership training at his church and create original curriculum for a step on their discipleship pathway. Mike found there's more to the Christian life than he realized.

Focus on the Goods, Not the Train

We want to be very clear that incorporating a small group structure into the ministry of your church is not the answer to revitalization. It is merely a vehicle that can transport life transforming relational discipleship from the dock to the marketplace, like a train that transports goods to consumers. If you load your small groups with curriculum or superficial fellowship, they will not accomplish the purpose for which they were designed. Therefore, the leadership of the church must guard against small groups veering off course in the direction of Bible study or social activity. If they do, they will lose their potency and lives will not be changed. Within a few years you will see a decline in participation because people will come to believe small group involvement is just another activity squeezed into an already overcrowded schedule. The prevailing attitude toward small groups will be, "Been there, done that, and they don't really make any difference."

A prefect example of this type of decline of a once effective structure is the Sunday school movement. Sunday school originated in England in 1780, and eventually spread throughout Europe and the United States. Because religious instruction was usually given in regular European schools, Sunday schools were not as important as they were in the United States, where the separation of church and state prohibited religious instruction in public schools.[1] Out of this movement that swept through our country came thousands of preachers and missionaries, as well as a nation of people raised on biblical truth. However, by the middle of the twentieth century, the nationwide Sunday school movement was a mere shadow of its former self. It had worked in the past, but it was no longer making a life-changing difference. In many churches, Sunday school had devolved into perfunctory gatherings that plodded through irrelevant curriculum. The once effective format did not keep up with the culture, and church leadership focused on the train instead of the goods it was meant to carry. Week after week they sent an empty train to the marketplace. When consumers realized the train carried nothing of value, they stopped coming to the station. If the church does not keep small groups focused on relevant relational discipleship, they too will become an ineffective activity people disregard.

If you currently have existing small groups that focus on curriculum or social activity, you will want to refocus them on relational discipleship if your intention is to facilitate life transformation. Remember the objective of small groups: to provide an emotionally safe environment where a believer's spiritual agitation can be appropriately addressed.

If you are planning to establish small groups in your church, it is important to carefully plan their development and filter those plans through the criteria for effectiveness: Do these groups produce emotionally healthy biblical community and believers who explore their purpose and call? Some suggestions for launching small groups include:

[1]Encyclopedia Britannica

- For an excellent explanation of effective small group structure, read *Prepare Your Church for the Future* by Carl George (Baker Book House: Grand Rapids MI, 2000).

- There are several models of small group format from which to choose—geographic, neighborhood, lecture lab, affinity, etc. Do the research and discover the model that works best in your setting.

- A great resource for how to facilitate a small group is *Leading Life-Changing Small Groups* by Bill Donahue (Zondervan: Grand Rapids, MI, 1996).

- Research relevant small group curriculum you can recommend with confidence.

- Equip your small group leaders with a clear understanding of spiritual development (the ocean diagram) and how small groups fit into that process.

These steps will get you moving in the right direction. However, the most important suggestions we can make for keeping new or existing small groups focused on relational discipleship are these:

- In the context of small groups, church leadership should emphasize the benefit of connecting with others in biblical community and de-emphasize curriculum and fellowship.

- Small group leaders should be trained to emphasize relationships by asking the following two questions every time the group meets and allowing each member to respond:

1. What has happened in your life since we last met?

2. What is God saying to you?

These seem like fairly unassuming questions, but the impact they can have is enormous.

Question number one provides an opportunity to recap personal experiences that paint a picture of who people really are. It is in the course of this storytelling that the details of four major life areas are revealed: personal and family issues, personal ministry, spiritual disciplines, and self-defeating behaviors. This allows the group to use the relational tools employed by effective disciple makers—encouragement, receiving confession, direction and guidance, accountability and loving confrontation—and challenge them to step out of their comfort zones to discover God's purpose and calling. Re-read the story of Mike and Teri and you will see how these tools are effectively incorporated into small group interaction.

Question number two provides an opportunity to share what people believe God is revealing about their purpose and what it is to which God may be calling them. This allows the group to not only use the relational tools mentioned above in regard to their God-given purpose, but also to help interpret what God may be saying. In the midst of these deep, trusting relationships where people struggle together to understand the spiritual journey, they begin to hear God's voice more clearly.

Holly is a great example of how a small group can help clarify God's call. She had a fabulous voice and seriously considered pursuing a professional singing career. Many friends and family members encouraged her to go for it. She even went to the extent of pursuing an agent. But following this path further meant she would have to resign from the worship team at her church. Holly wasn't sure what God was telling her and, try as she might, she could not separate the sound of God's voice from her own. Holly confessed her confusion to her small group and together they wrestled through the ups and downs of clarifying God's call. The group encouraged her to find out more about a professional singing career, offered suggestions on how to obtain information, then assessed what she had gathered along with her. The group also held Holly's feet the fire when she got discouraged. "I just want to make a decision and get this over with!" she would cry in frustration. If Holly got stuck in a rut of negative thinking, the group would confront her and encourage her to keep moving ahead. Eventually, God's call to remain on the worship team became clear and Holly was able to put her thoughts of singing professionally on the shelf for now.

Once you have launched small groups that are focused on relational discipleship, how do you know if your groups are effective? Stories of personal transformation are reported and new ministry concepts emerge. You may hear someone say, "My small group saved my life! " or "My small group is the family I never had." People begin contacting church leaders and ask to discuss the ministries to which God is calling them.

There is a myth about small groups that they are for everyone all the time. That's simply not true. Forward movement characterizes a journey of faith (otherwise it is not a journey), and people move in and out of ministries as their spiritual needs dictate. As they move beyond their comfort zones and explore their purpose and call, they step into the unknown. They've come too far to go back, but they fear moving forward. Their small groups are filled with stage three travelers doing life together, but what people moving into stage four need are others who have traveled this road before to help interpret the signs along the way.

Objective of small groups: To provide an emotionally safe environment where a believer's spiritual agitation is appropriately addressed.

Criteria for small groups: Do these groups produce emotionally healthy, biblical community and believers who explore their purpose and call?

Measurement of effectiveness: Stories of personal transformation are reported and new ministry concepts emerge.

Opportunities to Go and See

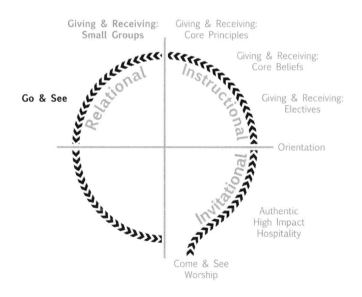

"By this time it was late in the day, so his disciples came to him. 'This is a remote place,' they said, 'and its already very late. Send the people away so they can go to the surrounding countryside and villages and buy themselves something to eat.' But he answered, 'You give them something to eat'" (Mark 6:35-37 NIV).

That's when the disciples essentially said to Jesus, "What? You've got to be kidding! We don't have enough money to feed all these people!" They sound like typical stage four travelers who have just had a head on collision with the fear barrier.

People at the fear barrier have persistently moved forward, worked through the confusing spiritual agitation that comes from confrontation with biblical truth, taken the risky step of moving beyond their comfort zones, and are now listening intently to hear what God wants them to do. When the message finally comes through loud and clear, they are often shocked and immediately question their own ability to accomplish the assignment. They don't believe they are capable and they don't have a clue about where to begin.

Annie and her husband, Mark, had served together on a worship team for years. He sang and she played the keyboard. We struck up a conversation one Sunday morning between services and I happened to mention we were thinking about a new position that would coordinate the multiple components of worship. Annie's eyes lit up and she said, "I might like to do that, but we would have to find someone to take over the keyboard." "Really?" I replied. "Why don't you pray about it and we'll talk more next week?" She agreed. Annie and I talked many times during the months that followed. She and Mark spent hours trying to discern God's plan. She agonized over the possibility of leaving the worship team and serving without Mark. They tossed around the idea of doing both, but didn't want her to become overloaded and burn out. We took her through a Keirsey Temperament Sorter® and StrengthsFinder® to help determine if she was appropriately wired for the position. I created a job description for her to consider and reviewed it with her in detail. I explained it described the responsibilities of a full time worship coordinator, but the position could be broken into smaller part time segments. I asked her to take it home and think about which responsibilities were of the most interest to her. I also explained we had not budgeted for this position in the current year and our intention was to begin with an unpaid servant, and then transition to a part time paid staff position that would eventually move to full time.

At that time, Annie worked part time at a local coffee shop, but had grown increasingly frustrated with her job. She couldn't leave, however, until she found another job to replace the income. She had longed to be in full-time ministry, and now she found herself confronted with an opportunity to do something she loved, but it would have to be without pay. Annie became more frustrated with her job at the coffee shop, more confused about the new opportunity to coordinate worship, and the agitation continued to build. She lay awake at night thinking through the options. She was exhausted and strung out like a piano wire.

Annie finally called and we set an appointment to meet and talk through the options. It was time to make a decision. As soon as we sat down to talk, Annie burst into tears. She sobbed through an explanation of their need for her income; how much she disliked her current job; that she couldn't possibly do both her job and coordinate worship; that she didn't know if she was capable of doing everything we expected. When she had finally exhausted her words, I reminded her that she could try out only those responsibilities she was most interested in. This was not an all or nothing proposition. There was the flexibility and freedom to take this position for a test drive. We wanted her to go and see what she was capable of doing as a worship coordinator, and then we could make a more permanent decision about the future. "I don't know if I can do some of the things on the job description," she confessed. "That's not a problem." I countered. "You won't be doing this alone. I will work with you until you feel like you can do it on your own." I encouraged Annie to go home, continue praying, talk things over with Mark, and get back with me in a few days with her decision.

Annie returned three days later and said, "I know what I want to do. I want to coordinate our Easter worship celebrations. Not the services every Sunday, just the services for Holy Week. Mark and I talked about it and I think I can do this and my job as well, and we'll see how it goes." Annie was right. She didn't know how to do some of the things that were required of her, but she learned. We met weekly to plan what she would do in the coming week and evaluate what she had done the week before. We talked through the obstacles she encountered and celebrated together when her efforts produced great results. Annie's feet were off the bottom and she was learning to swim in deeper water.

Let's recap the progression of events with Annie and identify what an opportunity to "go and see" looks like:

1. The church adopted a philosophy of filling ministry leadership with those whom God calls to serve, instead of merely filling a position with anyone who was available and willing or who had the skills but lacks the call.

2. The church moved slowly.

   - The servant was given time to determine if God was calling her to this ministry and work through the internal gyrations that come with discerning God's voice.

   - The leadership took time to assess the servant's strengths and weaknesses to help determine if she was a good match with the responsibilities of the ministry and the team with which she would be working.

3. The church was upfront with the sacrifices the servant would have to make to serve in ministry leadership. In the case of Annie, the sacrifice was serving with no pay and additional hours over and above her job at the coffee shop.

4. The church was flexible. Instead of insisting that a servant take on all the responsibilities or nothing, the position could be divided into manageable components, and the servant was encouraged to help decide how to divide the responsibilities into bite size pieces.

5. The church made the servant an "apprentice" first and trained her in philosophy and implementation that aligns with the expectations of the church's leadership.

6. The church not only allowed for but also encouraged the servant to "test drive" the ministry position before making a long-term decision.

The church is notorious for putting people into ministry and walking away. They are left to sink or swim. If it works, that's great. If it doesn't work, we just find someone else who is willing to try. Maybe this one won't sink! But that's not the way Jesus launched people into ministry. First, he did ministry while they watched. Second, they did ministry together. Third, they did ministry while he watched. All the while, he interpreted their experiences. When they ran into an obstacle, he talked them through it as in this story of the feeding of the 5,000. He prepared them for the suffering that would come as a result of following him. He cautioned them to remain focused and disciplined so Satan would not devour them. Finally, they did ministry on their own without him, and in doing so spread the Gospel around the world. This is the pattern the church must follow if our desire is to move people through the fear barrier to a place where they are no longer just believers but followers of Christ. The primary ministry to people at stage four is providing opportunities to go and see what they are capable of accomplishing for God. Success or failure is not the issue at this stage. The objective is to provide an accurate understanding of God, self, purpose, and call.

Interpret Their Experience

Stage four believers need someone to help interpret their thoughts, feelings, and emotions. They are looking for someone to lead the way and help them understand everything they are experiencing. That means the church must recruit people who have already moved through fear and experienced the journey ahead. That may be a senior staff person to whom all those struggling through stage four are directed. It may be small groups designed specifically to move people through stage four. Whatever form your "go and see" opportunities take, the following issues must be addressed:

- They need to know they are not crazy, and that the agitation and confusion they are experiencing is typical for this stage of spiritual development.

- They need an overview of the journey ahead so they have a point of reference as they continue forward.

Bruce Wilkerson's book, *The Dream Giver* (Multnomah: Sisters, OR, 2003) has been an invaluable resource in addressing these issues.

Prepare Them for the Road Ahead

Stage four believers need to develop an accurate understanding of who they are and the unresolved issues that have the potential to undermine their ministry. This will require a trusting relationship between the person at stage four and the discipler who leads him or her. At this point, mere friendship will cause the would-be discipler to go easy on his or her friend for fear of being disliked. There must be a willingness on the part of the discipler to lay it all on the line, and on the part of the disciple to receive the honest truth, take a ruthless personal inventory, and resolve self-defeating patterns. Peter Scazzaro's book, *The Emotionally Healthy Church*, can provide a framework for creating a church culture in which this type of self-reflection and assessment is embraced and encouraged.

They also need to develop an accurate understanding of God's perspective on those topics that can become barriers in stages five and six, including suffering, focus, discipline, and isolation. If they misinterpret the suffering that comes with following Christ and take it personally, they will abort their mission before it is accomplished. If they lose focus and allow themselves to be distracted by personal or ministry related matters that pull them away from God's calling; if they are undisciplined in their personal or work habits; if they allow themselves to become isolated, they will abort the mission. Equip people in advance to avoid these barriers to forward movement and the journey that lies ahead. You may find existing material that addressed each of these topics, or you may research and develop original curriculum to use in your go and see opportunity.

Help Them Follow God's Call

Create a permission giving culture that allows people to openly wrestle with God's call without fear of reprimand for not behaving like a "good Christian." The senior pastor and senior staff create such a culture by adopting a philosophy of authenticity then modeling it, preaching it to the church family, teaching it to the staff and ministry leaders, and establishing management structures that provide for accountability to insure staff and ministry leaders are also modeling an authentic lifestyle. When the senior staff makes it a practice to speak honestly about strengths, weaknesses, successes, and failures, and not take themselves too seriously, they set a tone that is carried throughout the entire congregation, and people are free to be themselves. Also, train ministry and small group leaders to recognize the characteristics of people at stage four and release them to move on when the situation dictates.

Beth is a children's ministry leader who meets weekly with her key servants. Her administrative assistant, Carolyn, had been struggling to clearly hear God's voice. She had strong administrative skills and thought serving in children's ministry would be a good fit but, after a year, she wasn't happy. She seemed to sense God had something else in mind. Beth noticed that Carolyn was more quiet than usual. She found her on the verge of tears several times, and Carolyn was not as enthusiastic about the tasks she once found exciting. At their weekly meeting, Beth began by gently talking with Carolyn about her observations. Because they had met weekly for twelve months, a foundation of trust had been built. The leadership had created a culture of authenticity, so Carolyn felt comfortable confessing the truth about her internal agitation. Beth assured Carolyn God would provide for the administrative needs of the ministry, and the most important thing for Carolyn was to pursue God's call. Carolyn continued to work with children's ministry while she talked with the director of mission and outreach about her strong desire to connect with missions. As God's call clarified, Beth released Carolyn to serve as the mission coordinator and, just as she said, God provided other servants to take her place.

Create a culture of ministry exploration that encourages "test drive" opportunities in each ministry area. People fear committing fully to something that may be a bad fit. Allowing them to test the water before they dive in creates an environment where exploration is acceptable. (Chapter Thirteen will discuss test drive opportunities in more detail.)

Establish an expectation that ministry leaders will develop discipling relationships with the people who serve on their teams. These expectations should not only be spoken, but also modeled by senior leadership. To create a culture where discipling relationships are commonplace, staff supervisors should adopt the following practices when meeting with their ministry leaders:

- Conduct regular one-on-one meetings. The frequency with which you meet should be determined by the amount of responsibility carried by each ministry, and how quickly they need updated information to effectively accomplish their job. For example, meeting every week with the facilities management team leader will keep him or her abreast of upcoming building usage. It may be appropriate to meet every other week with the team leaders of office administration or finances. Monthly meetings may be appropriate for technical team leaders, such as computer support, media operation, sound, and lighting. It may only be necessary to meet quarterly with team leaders for first time visitor follow up, or with the ushers and greeters so they know what to expect with upcoming holidays or special worship services. The key is to schedule dates and times in advance, establish a pattern, and meet regularly.

Conduct your time together in a conversational manner. Opportunities to support, encourage, offer direction and guidance, and cast vision arise in the give and take of conversation. Trust building and accountability happens by asking your leader specific questions about themselves *before* you ask about his or her ministry.

- What's going on with you personally and with your family?
- What has God been saying to you?
- What's happening in your ministry?

Once your leaders are accustomed to this type of discipling relationship, set the expectation that they will incorporate the same type of relationship into their own ministry areas.

There are steps a church must take to become an intentional disciple making church that empowers people in stages four, five and six to fulfill their purpose and call. As you develop opportunities to go and see, filter your plans through the criteria for effectiveness: Do these opportunities actually launch people toward living out their call? You may share a lot of wonderful insights with people at stage four, but you are not succeeding if the opportunities you offer do not move them forward in their ability to fulfill their God-given purpose.

How do you know if your efforts are effective? People are encouraged by the church to experiment before they commit to service and they personally demonstrate courage to take new ministry risks. You know you are encouraging people to experiment if you allow them to resign from a ministry without coaxing them to continue. If you

> **Objective of go and see:** To provide an accurate understanding of God, self, purpose and call.
>
> **Criteria for go and see:** Do these opportunities actually launch people toward living out their call?
>
> **Measurement of effectiveness:** People are encouraged by the church to experiment before they commit to service and personally demonstrate courage to take new ministry risks.

remember that the creator of the universe doesn't actually need our help and let them walk away in pursuit of their true calling, you can claim success in the first part of this measurement. The second part is quantitative: How many people are actually moving into risk-taking service? That means they are stepping out in faith in identifiable ways and making a significant sacrifice to serve the mission of Christ.

Facing the fear barrier is not a once-in-a-lifetime occurrence. Once people move through it, the new places of risk have the potential for becoming their new comfort zones. When that happens, God will challenge them to move into deeper water where their feet will again come off the bottom. Those who commit to a lifetime of following Christ will find themselves at this place over and over again.

CHAPTER THIRTEEN

Servant Discipleship

In the last chapter, we examined how opportunities to go and see meet the needs of people at stage four. This final section of the pathway—servant discipleship—targets men and women in stages five and six. In spite of the fact that the majority of servants who fill our ministries and serving teams are new or rededicated believers in stage three, we have intentionally not addressed opportunities for them to serve. Until people reach stages four, five and six, serving should be de-emphasized while giving and receiving are given a higher priority. However, since people at all stages of spiritual development are typically conglomerated into the multiple serving opportunities a church has to offer, let's look at how each stage benefits from servant discipleship in a different way:

- Those at stage three are afforded the opportunity to serve out of a desire to help the church and contribute in a meaningful way;

- Those at stage four can test the water in various ministries as they seek to understand their purpose and call;

- Those at stages five and six are able to live out their calling in a safe, supportive environment.

It takes many people with a variety of gifts, talents, skills, and abilities at all stages of spiritual development to accomplish the mission of the church. As they serve together, a collective understanding of servanthood can progressively develop when church leadership is intentional about moving people toward spiritual maturity and their God-given purpose.

As people progress into stages five and six, servant discipleship specifically targets them with the objective of accurately interpreting the obstacles, temptations, and suffering that come with following God's purpose and call. Up-close, personal, and straightforward interpretation is necessary if mature followers who move into positions of leadership are to successfully maintain their focus and move a ministry forward.

Jane and Gary

Jane accepted Christ when she was a child. She was fully involved in church life growing up, married a Christian man, and raised three children. She and her husband, Lew, served in numerous ministries through the years, and Jane believed her primary role was to support her husband as he led Bible studies. She attended every session of every class he taught, and was Lew's biggest cheerleader.

When Jane and I crossed paths, spiritual agitation had her in a full body press against the fear barrier. She was a few short weeks from retiring after years of employment at a local factory, and wondered how she would live out the remainder of her days. At the same time, God was showing Jane a vision of serving the church through hospitality, and it was obvious she was to lead the way into a new ministry. The very thought of such an undertaking terrified her. She had always played second fiddle and did not consider herself a leader. However, with much anxiety, Jane accepted God's challenge.

From the start, Jane willingly surrendered to accountability. She sought direction and guidance when she encountered obstacles. She put all her efforts into the mission of the new ministry. There were times when she lost focus and had to be redirected. She learned to correctly interpret the suffering she encountered when her role as wife and mother changed as the result of leading a growing ministry. She learned to discipline herself to function as a leader after spending most of her adult life following others. The ministry grew to provide authentic high impact hospitality through food service for multiple ministries, numerous events, and over 650 worshippers each week. When Jane became thoroughly overwhelmed with the enormous responsibilities of her position, she analyzed the causes, confronted her self-defeating behaviors, and moved forward with a new perspective. Because Jane has an intimate relationship with the Holy Spirit and surrenders to ongoing accountability, she has blossomed into an effective leader with a flourishing ministry.

Jane internalizes all she learns from effective preachers, teachers, small group leaders, and the biblical community to which she is committed. Consequently, she thrives in the deep because she has willingly allowed God to slowly transform her character into one that more closely resembles the character of God. Notice that her character is the defining factor, not her performance-related skills.

Gary's story doesn't end as happily. He had served here and there in minor roles throughout the church, and he jumped at the chance to lead when an opportunity presented itself. Gary considered himself a mature Christian, and could articulate God's clear call to launch a men's ministry. He had previously led a similar ministry at another church, and felt he was competent to get the job done. Gary's staff supervisor presented him with the church's vision for men's ministry and he enthusiastically indicated he shared the same vision. They seemed to be on the same page, but, as time went by, warning signs that Gary was an unequipped leader began to appear. Although he was given a written job description, he fulfilled only those responsibilities he enjoyed and neglected everything else. He was impatient with church policies and repeatedly tried to maneuver around them. He would verbally agree with a course of action established by his ministry's leadership team, but would move in a completely different direction instead. He pitted team members against each other by complaining to some that others made unreasonable demands on his time. He resented and resisted direction and guidance from his supervisor, and criticized the church leadership to people who served on his team. Gary invested a great deal of time in the ministry, but complained about the personal sacrifices required to move it forward. Although he was skilled in the tasks of the ministry, Gary was difficult to work with and people could not trust him to follow through on commitments. Gary resigned when his supervisor confronted him about his self-defeating behaviors.

Gary had never properly equipped himself for the journey beyond stage four. Although he possessed many of the skills needed to perform the various tasks of the ministry, he had not developed personal character that reflects servanthood. Christlike character is a necessity for any stage five follower who has the desire to go and make effective ministry happen. As Gary attempted to move into deeper water, he was unable to navigate, and the ministry to which God called him failed to survive.

Choosing to serve and choosing to be a servant are vastly different. Choosing to serve is a performance-based decision. Do I have time in my schedule to accomplish the task? How long will it take to perform? How difficult is it? Will there be others helping me? Is this something I already know how to accomplish? These are questions typically asked by people moving through earlier stages of spiritual development as they attempt to match their current skills and availability with the task. However, as people reach stage five, there should be evidence that their character has taken on an attitude of servanthood that neither depends on their own skills, nor expects convenience. They should demonstrate an understanding that we are called to serve God by making our lives available for God's purposes in spite of our own convenience and comfort.

The story of Mary and Martha in Luke 10:38-42 (NRSV) speaks to this difference:

> "(Jesus) entered a certain village where a woman named Martha welcomed him into her home. She had a sister named Mary who sat at the Lord's feet and listened to what he was saying. But Martha was distracted by her many tasks; so she came to him and asked, 'Lord, do you not care that my sister has left me to do all the work by myself? Tell her then to help me.' But the Lord answered her, 'Martha, Martha, you are worried and distracted my many things; there is need of only one thing. Mary has chosen the better part which will not be taken away from her.'"

Mary is described as being "distracted by her many tasks." Later, Jesus points out that she is "worried and distracted by many things." According to *The Complete Wordstudy Dictionary: New Testament* by Spiros Zodhiastes (AMG Publishers: Chattanooga, TN, 1992), the first use of the word we translate into English as "distracted" is a Greek word meaning something being dragged around. In other words, Martha was being dragged around by her tasks; they were burdensome. The second use is a Latin word, "turbid" meaning turmoil, as in foreign particles being stirred up like sediment in muddy water. What Jesus observed in Martha was a person serving out of a heart filled with unresolved issues that, when stirred up, resulted in complaining and resentment. The "better part" Mary chose was the continued development of her character through an intimate relationship with Jesus.

Servant Discipleship

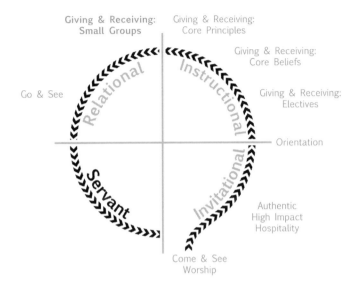

Giving & Receiving: Small Groups

Giving & Receiving: Core Principles

Giving & Receiving: Core Beliefs

Go & See

Relational

Instructional

Giving & Receiving: Electives

Orientation

Servant

Invitational

Authentic High Impact Hospitality

Come & See Worship

Servant discipleship creates opportunities for men and women to receive ongoing encouragement, direction, guidance, accountability and loving confrontation while using their performance-related gifts, talents, skills and abilities to fulfill the assignments God has given them. This combination of character building and mission-driven ministry involvement allows stage five followers to become more than foot soldiers in the army of God. They have the opportunity to become spiritual warriors.

In his book, *The Lost Art of Disciple Making* (Zondervan: Grand Rapids, MI, 1978), Leroy Eims defines a disciple as one who "takes his place among those who can vigorously and effectively advance the cause of the Lord. When that happens, he may be considered a mature, committed, fruitful follower of Jesus Christ" who makes a significant contribution not only by sharing knowledge and wisdom, but also by demonstrating spiritual depth and a godly life. Servant discipleship is the section of the pathway that helps those who have dared to move through the fear barrier capitalize on the knowledge and wisdom they have gained throughout their journey, and develop the disciplines and perspectives needed to live a spiritually mature life that makes a significant impact for Christ.

There are two components of servant discipleship: opportunities to go and make, and one-on-one discipling. Opportunities to go and make effective ministry under the direction and guidance of a discipler are the means by which stage five, new paradigm followers learn to remain focused and disciplined in spite of distractions. They also gain an accurate perspective of the suffering that will inevitably accompany their choice to follow God's call. One-on-one discipling helps guard stage six, fully committed followers against isolation that can result in the demise of the very ministry to which they are called.

Opportunities to Go and Make

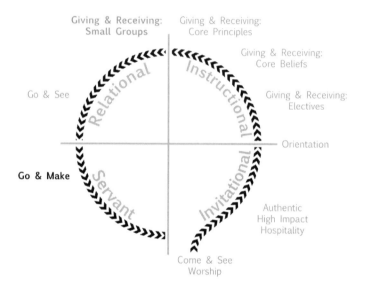

Moving into stage five is an incredibly intoxicating moment for new paradigm followers. They have broken through their fear barriers, and God has transformed their understanding of life and the world around them. The road ahead suddenly seems wide open, and they move forward with renewed energy. They brush against the reality that they truly have been uniquely created for a specific contribution to God's kingdom on planet earth. They can sense God's approval and blessing of their efforts, and begin to understand their value as individuals. But stage five is where the rubber meets the road. The challenges of ministry in the deep require discernment and clear interpretation so the hearts of people and their contribution to Christ's mission is not jeopardized.

Develop an Effective Ministry Structure

Organizational structure is the way in which interrelated groups are constructed for the purpose of effective communication and coordination. A well-organized ministry structure, where everyone who serves is connected to a line of accountability, is the relational foundation for effective go and make ministry opportunities.

Churches often resist conforming to structures that work well in secular organizations because they don't want to "turn into a corporation" that they perceive as cold, uncaring, and irreligious. Structures, however, do not determine spiritual integrity. It is what we do within the structures we create that shows the world our Christian character or lack thereof. A traditional denominational structure may work well in your particular setting. However, if it does not provide for appropriate accountability and you are experiencing poor communication and coordination of ministry efforts, your effect on the world around you will be significantly hampered. In other words, if you find yourself constantly frustrated because the left hand doesn't know what the right hand is doing; if things seem to never get done; if doing ministry is like spinning in circles, you need to take a long, hard look at your organizational structure and make the changes necessary to accomplish the mission to which the church as been commissioned.

In the church where we serve, ministries are organized in an arrangement commonly used by many companies and institutions.

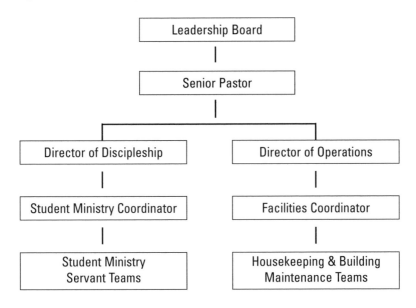

Obviously, this is a highly abbreviated version of our total organizational structure, but it provides a glimpse of the flow of communication and coordination that exists. As you can see, the senior pastor is accountable to a leadership board. Paid director level staff is accountable to the senior pastor. Paid and unpaid coordinator level ministry leaders are accountable to a staff director. Those who serve in ministries are accountable to ministry coordinators.

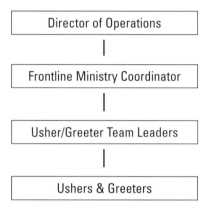

In larger ministries, servants may be accountable to coaches or team leaders who, in turn, are accountable to the ministry leader. For example, in a church with multiple worship services, one person (the frontline ministry coordinator) may supervise the usher and greeter ministry. He or she may have one team leader who recruits and schedules for each service. In that case, the ushers and greeters do not report directly to the coordinator, but to their respective team leader.

Creating a flowchart such as the ones shown above will allow you to see how your ministry leaders relate to staff and each other. If you create a chart showing how communication and accountability actually happen in your church today, you may begin to discover where your current structure is blocking your ability to accomplish effective ministry. Creating a flowchart of how your ministries ideally could be reorganized for greater effectiveness will give you a map for improved accountability, communication and ministry coordination, as well as identify positions for which you should recruit and/or hire.

Spend time researching how other effective churches organize their ministries to find the structure that will work best in your setting. The implementer with whom we encouraged pastors to partner in chapter eight is a good resource person to help determine whether or not your existing organizational structure is built for effective ministry. When an effective ministry structure is established, those who serve more clearly understand their place in the body of Christ. This understanding contributes to greater unity. Less confusion and conflict arise when unity prevails. Confusion and conflict are two great dangers lurking in the deep waters of the church, with the potential to destroy ministry. It is the responsibility of senior leadership to make every effort to overcome and minimize anything that hinders the forward progress of Christ's mission.

Create a Culture of Servanthood

To effectively minister to people at this stage, a culture of servanthood must permeate the entire church, and interpretation of obstacles must be an intentional act built into the ministry structure.

Developing a culture of servanthood is a multi-step process that will take many months to accomplish. It involves far more than simply calling people servants. Creating a culture involves the re-education of your church family through the introduction of new understandings and perspectives. By consistently championing these new ideas over an extended period of time, they begin to take root the same way marketing campaigns take root in our thinking after repeatedly hearing advertising slogans.

Lead Out of Brokenness and Vulnerability

Servanthood starts at the top of the leadership pyramid, with the senior pastor setting the course for the rest of the congregation. In *The Emotionally Healthy Church: A Strategy for Discipleship that Actually Changes Lives*, author Peter Scazzero says:

"In emotionally healthy churches, people live and lead out of brokenness and vulnerability. They understand that leadership in the kingdom of God is from the bottom up, not a grasping, controlling, or lording over others. It is leading out of failure and pain, questions and struggles—a serving that lets go. It is a noticeably different way of life from what is commonly modeled in the world and, unfortunately, in many churches."

That means the senior leadership is open and honest about their weaknesses, shortcomings, and God's amazing redemptive work in their lives. If the senior pastor struggles with a need to have people like her, incorporate the sharing of that weakness into sermons. If the director of discipleship is not gifted with strong administrative skills, partner with a strong implementer instead of trying to muddle through alone. If the director of operations is living in his second marriage, acknowledge the failure of the first marriage and the power of God's grace to restore his brokenness. We have all sinned and fallen short of the glory of God. When we acknowledge that truth and live out of God's strength and not our own, the church family begins to equate servant-hood with leadership and willingly follows the example set before them.

Speak the Language of Servanthood

The church is part of a kingdom, not a democracy. Scripture calls us to serve our King, to perform the duties to which we have been assigned. That means we are called to be servants. Unfortunately, we tend to solicit volunteers. By definition, volunteers render a service but have no fiduciary interest in the transaction. In other words, they get the job done, but have no vested interest in the ultimate purpose for which they have performed the service. They may accomplish the task, but their self-interest prevents them from transforming lives. If what we seek are committed servants, we have to use language that reflects the reality of what we are hoping to accomplish.

Begin by changing the understanding of paid staff about servant-hood through one-on-one conversations and staff meetings. The staff is perceived by the church family to be guardians of the official stance of the church on any given issue. They interact with the church family from positions of authority and have the ability to influence others. Therefore, you want them to be carriers of the message you wish to convey to the congregation, not only through their conversations, but also through written communications such as newsletters, bulletins, fliers, etc.

Reflect servanthood in your communication to the congregation. For example, replace the word "volunteer" with the word "servant" and the words "work" and "help" with "serve." When verbal and written communication no longer says, "We are looking for volunteers to help teach children's Sunday school or work in the nursery" but instead says, "We are seeking servants to serve in children's Sunday school or the nursery" the message of servanthood will begin to sift into congregational thinking. These may seem like minor changes, but the language of the church family will slowly begin to change, and with it will come the beginning of a new church-wide perspective.

Speak the Language of Calling

To develop a culture of servanthood, create opportunities for people to clarify their purpose and call. Speak from the pulpit, in classes, and in meetings about hearing and obeying God. Ask people what God is saying to them. Offer classes that help people understand their unique purpose, their God-given strengths, and spiritual gifts. The more you communicate the importance of hearing God and discovering God's purpose for each individual, the more your congregation will begin to move in the direction of becoming God's servants.

Create Value in Your Servants

Devalued servants begin to feel like slaves. No one wants to serve under oppression and they won't. They will leave. Therefore, it is critical to create value in your servants. Recognition is nice but, in our experience, those who are truly servants of God are not flattered by public recognition. Sincere individualized recognition for their efforts carries more meaning but there are more far reaching steps a church must take to let their people know they matter.

People feel valued when they believe they have genuinely been seen and heard. Valuing a servant is demonstrated in four primary ways:

REMOVE OBSTACLES TO MINISTRY

Can your servants *easily* gain access to your building, rooms, and common areas when necessary? Do they have *easy* access to the copier, office supplies, a computer and printer? Can they *easily* access tables, chairs, and A/V equipment? Are they able to communicate with key staff people through voicemail, email, or accessible mailboxes? Is the office open during business hours when those who work in the marketplace need to reach someone at the church? Do they know their ministry budget? If you answered no to any of these questions, you are probably discouraging your servants by handcuffing their efforts to go and make effective ministry happen. People feel valued when you equip and empower them to serve.

EXPECT DECISIONS TO SERVE TO BE BASED ON GOD'S LEADING, NOT ON TASKS TO BE ACCOMPLISHED

People feel valued when they are given time to prayerfully consider their decision to serve. Encourage them to say yes only if they believe it is what God wants them to do. When they know they have permission and the freedom to say no, they believe the church genuinely cares about them.

Offer a variety of opportunities and multiple ways to serve. For cxamplc, wc conduct an annual servant sign-up. The pastor preaches a series of sermons dealing with servanthood. On the first Sunday of the series, we distribute catalogs listing every ministry opportunity the church has available are distributed with the bulletins and also made available in the lobby. People have several weeks for prayerfully consideration. We designate the last Sunday of the series Servant Commitment Sunday, when everyone is given a commitment card to complete. They can choose from the following options:

- test-drive a ministry opportunity;

- make a new one-year commitment to serve;

- renew a commitment to continue serving in a ministry;

- talk with a staff person to help clarify their purpose and call;

- describe a "God dream" they believe they are called to personally develop and lead.

Test-drive opportunities allow people to meet with a ministry leader and either observe ministry in action, or serve one time before they make a commitment. By creating a culture where test-drives are part of the norm, people begin to understand the church is seeking those whose service is aligned with their God-given purpose, not just warm bodies who are willing to get the work done.

GIVE AUTHORITY ALONG WITH RESPONSIBILITY

People feel valued when you genuinely entrust them with both responsibility and authority. Giving authority means you allow the person to whom you have given the responsibility to carry it out without destructive interference by you or someone else. People driven by God's call are compelled to serve. When they are shackled by destructive interference and begin to suffocate, they will seek out a place where they can to breath and serve unhindered.

To prevent destructive interference, the senior pastor, staff and senior leadership must learn to demonstrate self-control.

- **Don't micro-manage.** Micro-management happens when you ask for an account of the intricate details of how the task will be accomplished, and critique each detail instead of entrusting the details to the servant. Micro-management looks like this: You entrust a ministry leader with a task in which he or she has shown competence or expertise. Instead of allowing that person to work out the details of the task and bring you a finished product, you either tell him or her how you want the details worked out, or you constantly ask about the details and critique each one. You will emotionally wear that person to a frazzle and he or she will eventually leave your church. Remember the dead bodies that wash back on shore? This is a primary source of those cadavers.

- **Don't violate chain of command.** You break chain of command when you answer for the person to whom you have given responsibility, instead of directing others back to him or her.

Let's say you're the pastor and you have a student ministry leader named Jim who is accountable to you. You have given Jim responsibility for all ministry to students in grades seven through twelve. Mary comes to you with an idea for a senior high Sunday school class. Do you say, "What a great idea! What curriculum are you planning to use? What time did you want to have that class? We can put it in the bulletin next week." Or do you say, "What a great idea! I'd like you to get in touch with Jim, our student ministries leader. He's responsible for that." If you do anything other than send Mary directly to Jim, you are breaking chain of command and undermining Jim's authority. From that point on, Mary will understand that Jim has no power and she will continue to come to you. This happens all the time in the church and is justified as "helping." In reality, breaking chain of command devalues and discourages ministry leaders.

Sometimes people simply don't want to follow the appropriate channels. "But Pastor, I just can't talk to Jim. I'd much rather talk with you." What do you do? You send that person to Jim anyway. You, your staff, and your senior leadership are responsible for retraining your people by establishing a new set of expectations.

Ongoing, uncorrected violations of the chain of command will constantly keep servants confused and suspicious. Eventually, they will leave your church bruised, battered, and looking for a place to hide and heal their emotional wounds.

- **Don't abdicate.** There are some in senior leadership who actually err in the opposite direction by abdicating instead of delegating responsibility and authority. That means they turn over responsibility to a leader, give the leader authority to carry out the assignment, and that's the end of that. The ministry leader never hears from anyone higher up in the chain of command again. They receive nothing: no direction or guidance; no encouragement or accountability; no feedback of any kind. That ministry leader isn't even a blip on the screen of those in senior leadership who are guilty of abdication. If there is any contact at all, it is because the ministry leader pursues someone to provide constructive feedback that is essential to the development of healthy, effective ministry. Because the ministry leader is left to sink or swim alone, he or she cannot maintain an objective perspective, becomes discouraged, and the ministry eventually flounders or fails.

SCHEDULE REGULAR OPPORTUNITIES FOR FEEDBACK AND DISCUSSION

A person at stage five who is following God's call needs time to give and receive feedback and discuss:

- personal and family issues;

- spiritual issues;

- ministry related tasks.

The last thing they need, however, is superficial feedback that focuses solely on the task-related outcome. How did your servant appreciation event turn out ? Did everyone have a good time? Are you going to do one again next year?" And then the conversation drifts off to something unrelated that's happening elsewhere in the church or community.

When a person at this stage is attempting to intentionally grow in their faith, they need feedback with some meat on its bones! They want honesty and objectivity; they want to be challenged to be the best they can be. "I watched you lead the Easter worship brainstorming session and I have some observations to make. You did a great job drawing out ideas but I believe you can enhance your credibility with the worship team if you make a slight adjustment. Do you remember when you asked for ideas to write on the flip chart? You didn't write down every idea. That makes the people whose ideas were overlooked feel unimportant. It's vital to the process to write down every idea no matter how good or bad you may think it is. Everyone will appreciate your fairness and be much more willing to share. What do you think?" This type of constructive feedback leads into authentic conversations in which obstacles, temptations, and suffering that come with following God's purpose and call come to light. It's then up to the staff supervisor who functions as a discipler to drive the conversation and interpret the circumstances. Authentic accountability between a ministry leader and a staff supervisor looks like this:

- They meet weekly, monthly or quarterly depending on the ministry.

- The staff supervisor asks the following:

  1) In what areas have you made progress since our last meeting?

  2) In what areas are you having difficulty?

  3) What events do you have coming up and what is the status of each?

  4) What decision or input do you need from me?

  5) Tell me about the leaders in your ministry? (if there are any)

     a. What indicates growth in their faith?

     b. What indicates growth in their leadership skills and abilities?

     c. How are you maximizing their gifts and talents?

6) What intentional steps are you taking to grow as a ministry leader?

7) How are you personally?

    a. Tell me about your spiritual life? Where are you succeeding? Where are you experiencing difficulties?

    b. Tell me about your family? Where are you succeeding? Where are you experiencing difficulties? What are you doing to balance family and ministry?

Authentic accountability that offers constructive feedback creates value in individuals because they know they have been seen and heard. They know their worth is measured by something greater than what they are capable of producing.

EXPECT MINISTRY LEADERS TO VALUE THEIR TEAMS

For this new culture to permeate the entire church, senior leadership must interpret servanthood to ministry leaders and establish an expectation that they, in turn, will interpret it to the men and women who serve in their ministries.

CHOOSE BIBLICALLY CALLED LEADERS

Discernment on the part of senior leadership in the selection of ministry leaders is critical to effective ministry. Careful selection will go a long way toward preventing damage caused by unequipped ministry leaders who lack an understanding of servanthood. Review the stories of Jan and Gary and you will see the difference.

First Timothy 3: 1-12 outlines the qualities of biblical leaders. They:

- Must first be tested. In other words they must willingly serve before being put into leadership and in so doing demonstrate biblical leadership qualities. If those qualities are not evident, they are not qualified to lead.

- Must not be a new believer.

- Must be:

  - trustworthy;

- self-controlled;

- hospitable;

- of sincere character;

- able to direct others;

- moral and ethical.

As you develop an effective ministry structure and create a culture of servanthood, keep in mind the criteria for effective go and make opportunities—obstacles to effectiveness caused by a lack of focus and discipline are overcome and people are empowered to fully live out their purpose and call. You know you are succeeding when those who are living out their purpose and call articulate encouragement and support from the church.

Mindy, her husband, and their three sons attended the same church in which she had grown up. It was located thirty miles away from where she lived, and God was nudging her to move to a church closer to home. She had just made a one-year commitment to serve in children's ministry but God was not impressed and insisted she make the change, so off they went in search of a new church. They began attending one with an excellent youth ministry and another with a new visionary preacher that recently began offering a contemporary service. It had a youth ministry that was far less vibrant than the other church they were considering. Besides that, the outdated, handmade pillows scattered here and there in the pews turned Mindy off.. When she asked an usher about them, he replied, "Oh, we've had those around for years. Some people like to lean back against them in the hard pews." "Do you see the awesome youth ministry at one church and old pillows at the other?" she asked God. "Please let me go to the church with the rockin' youth ministry." Once again, God was not impressed with Mindy's personal preferences and pointed her to "the pillow church." She reluctantly obeyed.

Mindy is an elementary teacher by profession so she made herself available to serve in children's ministry and, eventually, she launched an adult Sunday school class as well. The class consisted of the same dozen men and women from a congregation of 375 who met Sunday after Sunday to discuss different topical studies. She believed teaching in both children's ministry and adult Sunday school was a good fit that was in line with her gifts, talents, skills, and abilities. Besides, serving in these areas was safe and predictable.

That's when the new director of discipleship joined the staff. After several months of observing Mindy, he approached her with the challenge of facilitating a new class about the core beliefs of the Christian faith. This new class would not be a puddle—an ongoing class limited to the same twelve people—but would be instead a stream that would move different people through a six-week class that would be offered three times each year. What's more, he wanted Mindy to help him write original curriculum instead of using a study guide purchased at the local Christian bookstore. Mindy went through all the gyrations of someone moving through the fear barrier, having her feet come off the bottom and, for the first time in her life, depend on God to sustain her instead depending on her own skills. This time serving was not safe. It was unpredictable and she was way outside her comfort zone!

Mindy's biggest fear was that no one but her original twelve adult class members would want to attend after the first six-week session. Eight years after entering the "pillow church," and three and a half years after accepting the challenge to help create and facilitate the core beliefs class, the church has experienced significant growth, and Mindy has shared the experience with almost 150 people. She is now training a capable facilitator to take her place because she began sensing God's call to launch a women's ministry. In spite of her lack of experience in this particular area, Mindy is working closely with the director of discipleship as she ventures into this new arena. She recently told him, "You know, I could have lived the rest of my life quite comfortably serving in children's ministry and teaching Sunday school the way I had always done it. Instead, this church challenged me to go further, do more, and follow God into risky, unknown places. But I was never left hanging out there on my own, even when I hit some rough spots and wanted to give up. All along the way, I've received encouragement and support, and I'm having the adventure of a lifetime. I can't believe God is using me to launch a women's ministry. I'm excited and scared all at the same time . . . and I wouldn't trade this for anything in the world." That is the sound of success for a church striving to develop effective go and make opportunities.

> **Objective of go and make:** To accurately interpret the obstacles, temptations and suffering that come with following God's purpose and call.
>
> **Criteria for go and see:** Are obstacles, temptations and suffering overcome and people empowered to fully live out their purpose and call?
>
> **Measurement of effectiveness:** Those living out their purpose and call articulate encouragement and support from the church.

One-On-One Discipling

There are those who continue moving forward on their spiritual journeys and become stage six, fully committed followers. These are not the people who make up the majority of our congregations. These are the few whose entire life focus is to move the mission of Christ forward, no matter what. They may be paid or unpaid servants. They may be attached to the church, a parachurch organization, or the secular marketplace. They may or may not hold the official title of "leader," but they do, in fact, lead. They can't *not* lead because they are compelled by God's call to accomplish the assignments God has given them.

In the bestseller, *Good to Great*, author Jim Collins ranks leaders on a scale of one to five, with level five at the top. The following is a summary of leadership capabilities of level five leaders.

- They embody a paradoxical mix of personal humility and professional will.

- They are ambitious, to be sure, but first and foremost for the company, not themselves.

- Level five leaders set up their successors for even greater success in the next generation.

- Level five leaders display a compelling modesty, are self-effacing, and understanding.

- Level five leaders are fanatically driven and infected with an incurable need to produce sustained results.

- They resolve to do whatever it takes to make the company great, no matter how big or hard the decisions.

- Level five leaders display a workman-like diligence—more plow horse than show horse.

- Level five leaders look out the window to attribute success to factors other than themselves.

- When things go poorly, however, they look in the mirror and blame themselves, taking full responsibility.

If we replace the word "company" with "mission of Christ," we discover an accurate description of stage six, fully committed followers. It describes Peter and Paul, as well as the great men and women of the Christian faith we all admire, like Billy Graham and Mother Teresa. It also describes men and women whose names most of us will never know. Just as Collins found level five leaders in companies that have transitioned from good to great, so will we find in our own churches fully committed followers who are on a personal mission to advance the kingdom and move the impact of the church from good to great.

These people have moved through each stage of spiritual development and have developed a lifestyle of submission to the Holy Spirit as the Spirit molds and shapes their character to more closely resemble the likeness of Christ. "What do you want me to do, Lord?" is the primary question they ask in relation to every area of their lives. Biblical reason, instead of emotional, wants and desires direct their decisions. They live by First Corinthians 10:23-24, 31 (NIV):

> "Everything is permissible but not everything is beneficial. Everything is permissible but not everything is constructive. Nobody should seek his own good, but the good of others. So whether you eat or drink or whatever you do, do it all for the glory of God."

Their agenda is never personal but, instead, focused entirely on the mission. If you are intentional about meeting the discipling needs of those who have traveled to this stage of the journey, these men and women will take the ministry of your church to deeper levels of effectiveness than ever before.

Because fully committed followers are the minority and are single-mindedly focused on their God-given assignments, it becomes surprisingly easy for them to fall into isolation. Think about it: When we see a highly capable individual who is effecting lives right and left through highly effective ministry, what do we think to ourselves? "They've got it all together! They know exactly what they're doing and certainly don't need any help from me." Or we might take the route of spiritual inferiority. "That person has a very special connection with God. If I open my mouth, I will just sound ignorant. I could never speak with them at their level." So we cut them a wide berth and leave them alone because we have deluded ourselves into thinking they really don't put on their pants one leg at a time like the rest of us.

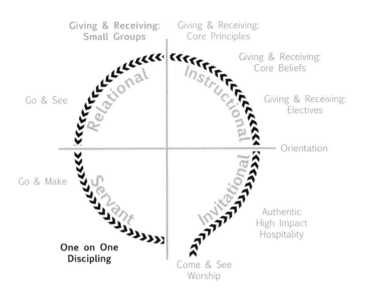

Isolation can also come from within the thoughts of a fully committed follower if the ego is not tamed. As others remain at arms length, a person at stage six can fall into thinking, "No one understands me. Nobody really gets what I'm trying to accomplish. I'm on my own, just God and me." With no objective input to help keep a stage six person from veering off course, isolation can increase to even more critical levels. When thoughts turn to a belief that "the rules don't apply to me," men and women who are extremely effective in ministry can find themselves on a slippery downhill slope. They can start believing that God has anointed them to the point where accountability is unnecessary. Because they are capable of producing incredible results, they can believe God will bless them no matter what they do.

An additional source of isolation comes from the perpetuation of the myth that "it's lonely at the top." My daughter was formerly employed as a professor at a large Bible college where she watched students come to believe that isolation is an inevitable part of full time ministry. Many professors who suffered from isolation themselves unintentionally conveyed the message to these young men and women that it is part and parcel of taking up your cross and following Jesus because it is all they've ever known. Pastors are particularly susceptible to this myth, and must intentionally guard themselves from the distorted perspective that comes from remaining isolated.

Whether isolation is the result of others keeping their distance and placing a fully committed follower on a pedestal, is self-imposed by an undisciplined ego, or is a myth mistaken for truth, the means by which people at this stage can remain on course is one-on-one discipling. The objective of one-on-one discipling is to provide ongoing, accurate interpretation of obstacles, temptations, and suffering so the pitfall of isolation can be avoided.

In Galatians 2:11-14a (NIV), Paul recounts a time when Peter chose a course of action based on his own emotional comfort rather than scriptural truth. Paul knew the cause of Christ could suffer a significant setback if Peter continued on his chosen course, but with the mission first and foremost in mind, Paul confronted him.

> "When Peter came to Antioch, I opposed him to his face, because he was clearly in the wrong. Before certain men came from James, he used to eat with the Gentiles. But when they arrived, he began to draw back and separate himself from the Gentiles because he was afraid of those who belonged to the circumcision group. The other Jews joined him in his hypocrisy, so that by their hypocrisy even Barnabas was led astray. When I saw that they were not acting in line with the truth of the gospel, I said to Peter . . ."

Paul goes on to recount his corrective action. Notice that "even Barnabas" followed Peter as he veered off course. Can't you hear Barnabas thinking to himself, "Peter's got it all together! He knows exactly what he's doing. Who am I to question one who actually walked with Jesus?" It's obvious none of the other believers were ready, willing, or able to step up to the plate and question Peter's actions. Only Paul had both the objectivity and fortitude needed to confront him one-on-one.

A fully committed follower (like Peter) needs another follower who is also fully committed (like Paul) to function in the role of discipler. Only someone who has experienced and overcome the barriers at each stage of the journey can truly relate to life in the deepest water. People at this stage have an extremely high level of commitment to the mission and expectation for themselves. Only someone who shares the same high level of commitment and expectation will have both the guts to confront and the credibility to effectively hold accountable another person at stage six. Someone with a lesser degree of commitment or expectation will have very limited credibility with a fully committed follower. Therefore, any well-intentioned advice offered might be politely received but disregarded as worthless. When a person of lesser commitment or expectation offers input based on emotion or personal agenda rather than the truth of the scripture, a fully committed follower will quickly discern the real impetus behind those recommendations and they will have no impact.

Kenneth Price in his book, *The Eagle Christian* (Old Faithful Publishing, 1989), describes the courting ritual of the Golden Eagle. It is a process by which the female eagle assesses the worthiness of the male to be her partner. It begins by the female grabbing a stick in her talons and flying high into the sky with the male eagle right on her tail. She rapidly descends in a series of figure eights, with the male still immediately behind her. Suddenly the female drops the stick and the male swoops to catch it. When he attempts to return it, however, the female is not interested because she has flown down to pick up a larger stick and begun the game again.

> "The male does not take her rejection to heart but returns the stick to the ground and falls in behind her as she ascends with a larger, heavier stick. And so the game continues. Each time she drops the stick, the male retrieves it. Each time she flies a little lower, a little faster and with a bigger stick. If the male ever fails to catch the falling stick, the female will chase him off and will not play anymore. The game climaxes when the female is flying at a tremendous speed in a nip and tuck figure eight, less than 500 feet from the ground releasing an object weighing almost as much as she weighs expecting the male to nab the log without crashing into the ground (he almost has to be an Olympic star). After finally satisfying the female that he is fit to be her husband, the eagles make their vows to one another."

Later in the book, Price describes how the female throws her eaglet out of the nest when it's time to fly. As the little one plummets to the ground, it begins to frantically flap its tiny wings. Just as the baby reaches the point of exhaustion and only a few thousand feet from the ground, the father swoops in and catches the little eaglet in his talons saving it from certain death. Herein lies the critical importance of the dating ritual. Both birds must be fully committed to the mission and share the same high expectations. There must be a high level of trust and mutual respect between them that allows them to partner together. It's the same for a stage six, fully committed follower and the one he or she selects to be a one-on-one discipler. Both must understand the experience of flying to new heights of ministry, as well as the obstacles that could cause a fatal crash at this stage, and they must share a mutual trust and respect that allows them to partner together.

When effective go and make opportunities are in place, a healthy ministry structure provides for accountability by a staff supervisor. But that supervisor may or may not be capable of functioning in the role of one-on-one discipler. However, when the church establishes an expectation of team ministry rather than "Lone Ranger" ministry, and supports it through structured accountability, it is upon this expectation that the church must capitalize to effectively meet the needs of stage six people. The senior leadership and their supervisor should encourage fully committed followers to find and partner with a discipler with whom they meet regularly, and then hold them accountable for doing so. A healthy stage six follower should actually demonstrate a desire for a running partner who can keep up the high powered pace and actively seek out such a person.

Fully committed followers should also be encouraged to stay involved with the authentic spiritual community—the people at various stages of development who demonstrate a sincere spiritual hunger—and be held accountable for that involvement as well. That means regular participation in worship and fellowship opportunities, discipling others who are sincerely seeking to grow in their faith, participating in conferences and seminars that expose them to fresh ideas and perspectives, etc.

The evidence of isolation becomes apparent when there is an imbalance between ministry and personal health that will be demonstrated in a variety of ways. The stage six person may constantly be too busy to interact socially with others. He or she may resist taking time away from ministry for personal renewal, in spite of weariness or exhaustion. If this person is married, there may be a noticeable, prolonged strain in the relationship with his or her spouse. If there are children, they may display noticeable and prolonged signs of deep unhappiness (not to be confused with typical teenage cynicism). Each of these is a potential red flag-warning that isolation may be creeping into the life of the fully committed follower. However, when effective one-on-one discipling is taking place, these issues are addressed on a regular basis with a trusted companion who can offer wise, objective, biblical counsel and help this person balance full impact ministry and holistic personal health.

The measure of success of a church's efforts to address the needs of fully committed followers is the evidence that they live and work at a deeper level of effectiveness that causes others to be drawn to and changed by the work of their ministry. People from the congregation will approach the senior leadership and testify to the personal transformation they have experienced as a result of the influence of a fully committed follower. That follower's name will be mentioned repeatedly as someone who has made a significant impact in the lives of many. That follower will receive numerous notes, letters, and emails expressing deep gratitude for the ministry they offer and the resulting transformation that has taken place. Other ministry leaders, both in your own church and from other churches, will often contact that stage six follower and ask to talk or meet with them to learn how they can become more effective.

The challenge to sustain effective ministry that produces long term results at stage six are huge, but so are the rewards. This is where the abundant life promised in scripture is realized. Through the ministry of a fully committed follower who avoids the pitfall of isolation, the blind receive sight, the lame walk, those who have leprosy are cured, the deaf hear, the dead are raised. and the good news is preached to the poor. The transforming power of the Holy Spirit may not manifest itself in the same way it did through the ministry of Jesus, but the life and ministry of a fully committed follower will bear the same fruit. Those who did not previously understand the truth will begin to understand, those who were previously unable to stand on their own spiritual and emotional feet will step up to the plate, those who viewed themselves as unclean will begin to understand their true value in the eyes of God, those who could not previously hear God's call on their lives will begin to recognize God's voice, those who once had no hope now find it through Jesus, and the disenfranchised begin to realize there is a place for them at the table.

Objective of one-on-one discipling: To provide ongoing, biblically accurate interpretation of obstacles, temptations and suffering so the pitfall of isolation can be avoided.

Criteria for go and see: Does this discipling effort move a fully committed follower toward a balance of full impact ministry and holistic personal health?

Measurement of effectiveness: Fully committed followers live and work at a deeper level of effectiveness that causes others to be drawn to and changed by the work of their ministry.

Epilogue

In *The Parable of the Dream Giver*[1],

" . . . Ordinary thought he heard the Dream Giver say, *Come further . . .* Ordinary found himself walking, knapsack over his shoulder, along the far wall at the back of the city. He noticed a little gate he'd never noticed before. He heard the Dream Giver again. *Come further.* He opened the gate and stepped outside. But as he did, he felt strangely . . . uncomfortable. He looked toward the distant Unknown. *Well done, Ordinary!* The Dream Giver said. *You are a good and faithful Dreamer. Now let me show you more.*"

Like Ordinary, the church is called to go further and develop even more than a discipleship pathway that moves adult men and women from unchurched to fully committed follower. It is called to apply the elements of each stage to virtually every ministry of the church by creating a discipleship pathway in children's ministry that moves boys and girls from unchurched to fully committed follower in age-appropriate ways. It is called to build a bridge from children's ministry to student ministry and create a discipleship pathway that moves teens and young adults from unchurched to fully committed follower. Every ministry should eventually demonstrate elements of come and see and authentic high impact hospitality if our hearts' desire is to make disciples of all nations.

Discipled followers are the key to health and unity in a growing church. The opposite is also true: Undiscipled followers are the key to un-health and disunity in a church that is experiencing no growth. We as church leaders must take the models given to us through scripture, intentionally apply them without apology, and demonstrate with our actions our desire to fulfill Christ's commission. We must become doers of the Word and not hearers only.

[1]Bruce Wilkerson, *The Dream Giver* (Multnomah: Sisters, OR, 2003).

The church is still God's hope for the world. Through Christ's church the manifold wisdom of God will be made known. It is God's intention for that to happen, therefore it will. If we want to be a generation that experiences the joy of God and see God's promises come to life, then we must begin today to boldly put our faith in God's ability to use us for decisive action. When we do, we will one day awaken to the reality of a renewed church. Not an irrelevant church struggling to get by, but a church that cannot be contained; a church that is so effectively used by God that the gates of hell will no longer stand against it.

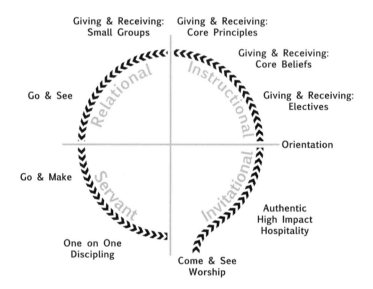